CECIL J. ALLEN

SALUTE TO THE

Southern

LONDON
IAN ALLAN LTD

First published 1974

Reprinted 1977

ISBN 0 7110 0471 4

Published by Ian Allan Ltd, Shepperton, Surrey and printed in the United Kingdom
by Morrison and Gibb Ltd, London and Edinburgh

Contents

Cover and centre page painting: Merchant Navy
class Pacific No. 35017 *Belgian Marine* heads the
"Bournemouth Belle" out of Waterloo in the
British Railways era, overtaking a suburban electric
multiple-unit on a Waterloo–Shepperton service.

▼ The nuisance of drifting exhaust with the Bulleid
Pacifics—No. 35012 *United States Lines* at speed near
Winchfield with a Bournemouth express.
[British Railways

1 · *Railway Beginnings in Southern England*

SMALLEST of all the four main line railways at the grouping in 1923, the Southern Railway was by no means the least influential. It had two chief claims to fame. One was the possession of what, by the end of its history, had become the biggest electrified suburban system owned by any one railway, not merely in Great Britain but in the whole world. The other was the scale of its maritime interests, both connecting this country with the Continent, but above all by its ownership of the port of Southampton.

Parliamentary powers for the construction of the first constituent of what a century later would become the Southern Railway were obtained in the same year as the opening of the Stockton & Darlington Railway—1825. The opening of this line coincided in 1830 with that of the Liverpool & Manchester Railway. It was the Canterbury & Whitstable Railway, 6 miles in length, designed to connect the cathedral city with the harbour at Whitstable. It had two very steep climbs, one at 1 in 28–31 up from the Whitstable direction to the flat central mile, and the other down at 1 in 41–56 into Canterbury, which had to be worked by stationary engines. In later years, however, with light trains, the line was capable of being worked throughout by steam locomotives. But special engines, severely restricted in dimensions, had to be used, as the Tylers Hill tunnel permitted a maximum height of 11ft only in the centre, and 9ft 3in at the two sides. Its first locomotive, the four-wheeled *Invicta*, is still preserved at Canterbury. The Canterbury & Whitstable Railway survived as a passenger-carrying line for precisely 100 years; freight traffic continued until after nationalisation, but the line closed down completely in 1952.

Actually the Surrey Iron Railway, opened in 1801, had long preceded the Canterbury & Whitstable, but the former was worked throughout its life by horses, and only one or two very short sections later provided the formation for steam-hauled trains. It was far away in the West Country that there next appeared a short line which eventually would form a part of the Southern system. It was a railway planned to unite the English and Irish Channels across the width of Cornwall from Fowey to Padstow, though eventually no more of it was built than the 7 miles between Bodmin and Wadebridge, with a 6½-mile branch to Wenford

Bridge, opened in 1834. Financial results were poor, and after a proposed acquisition by the Cornwall Railway (later the Great Western) had had no result, it was the London & South Western Railway, which already had its eyes on Devon and Cornwall (though the nearest point on its system at that time was 200 miles away!) that stepped in and purchased the tiny company. It was not until 1895, however, that the Bodmin & Wadebridge became physically connected to the LSWR by the opening of the latter's Delabole–Wadebridge section.

Next constituent of the future Southern Railway to come into existence was the first railway to enter London. This was the London & Greenwich, for which the Bill received the Royal Assent in 1833. The first section of the line, from Deptford to a temporary terminus at Spa Road, and finally to London Bridge, was ceremonially opened in December 1836; its 3¾ miles were carried throughout on brick arches, of which there were no fewer than 878 in all. Soon the principle of running powers was established by Parliament, for in 1835 the London & Croydon Railway was incorporated and obtained powers to use the Greenwich tracks from Corbett's Lane Junction to a London Bridge terminus of its own alongside that of the Greenwich company. Moreover, it was 1839 before the London & Croydon line was completed, and two years before that powers had been obtained for the London & Brighton Railway, which would obtain access to London Bridge over London & Croydon and Greenwich tracks.

Now a further complication arose. Parliamentary powers had been obtained in 1836 by a newly incorporated South Eastern Railway for a line from Norwood through Oxted to Tonbridge, Ashford and Folkestone to Dover, whose trains would use the same route into London Bridge. But the Brighton scheme of a year later offered the SER a new route; so powers were obtained by the latter company not only over the London & Croydon and Greenwich lines, but also over the London & Brighton line, when complete, as far as Reigate Junction, then later Redhill. From here the SER was to branch eastwards, with a main line that in 46 miles to Ashford would diverge by no more than a single mile from a dead straight course, then on to Folkestone, which was reached in 1843, and Dover a year later.

The remarkable thing now was that, after the London & Brighton and South Eastern companies had joined forces to build the line from Corbett's Lane as far as Redhill, with Parliamentary sanction they divided it between them, Brighton ownership extending as far as Coulsdon and South Eastern from there onwards. Right up to the grouping the latter remained SECR property, which was why, in 1900, the London, Brighton & South Coast completed and opened its own independent Quarry line from Coulsdon to Earlswood, by-passing Redhill altogether. The line from Redhill and Earlswood to Brighton had been completed in 1841.

Such was likely to be the congestion between Corbett's Lane Junction and London Bridge with four companies using the London & Greenwich tracks that the South Eastern Railway decided to have its own independent terminus, and in 1844 opened a branch from Corbett's Lane—which by now had become a junction of no small importance—to a new station at Bricklayer's Arms. A further reason was to avoid the exorbitant tolls that the Greenwich Company was exacting for the use of its lines. The London & Croydon shared in the cost of the branch, and some of its trains used the fine new station. But travellers found Bricklayer's Arms inconveniently far from the heart of the City, and less than three years after its opening passenger traffic into and out of it had ceased, though thereafter it was to become one of the most important goods stations on the South Eastern and eventually the Southern Railway.

Meantime, however, the position had been greatly simplified by the South Eastern in 1845 obtaining a lease for 999 years of the London & Greenwich. In the same year a new station was opened at London Bridge, with seven platforms and twelve tracks, and in 1847 powers were obtained to lay additional tracks between here and Corbett's Lane, which by 1850 had increased to six running roads. For a time there was considerable trouble at London Bridge through the London & Croydon station having been built on the north side of the Greenwich station, so that all trains into and out of the former had to cross the tracks of the latter, but eventually joint station working resolved the difficulty.

In the 1840s much attention was being devoted to atmospheric traction, as an alternative to steam. It had first been tried in Ireland, between Kingstown and Dalkey, and was favoured by such eminent engineers as Brunel and Cubitt, though Robert Stephenson and Locke were opposed to the idea. However, by the early 1840s the system was being seriously proposed for a number of railways then being planned in Southern England, and was actually introduced by the London & Croydon Railway between Dartmouth Arms (Forest Hill) and Croydon in the latter part of 1845. In order that there might be no interference with the through Brighton and South Eastern trains, a third track with the atmospheric equipment was laid parallel to the main line, and over this trains were run at half-hourly intervals, taking no more than 7min for the 5 miles. At Norwood the atmospheric line crossed the main line by the first railway flyover in the country.

At first things worked well, but soon, as was to happen shortly afterwards even more disastrously with Brunel's South Devon Railway, it was found impossible to keep airtight the leather flaps which closed the slots in the 15in suction pipe through which passed the connecting arms between the coaches and the pistons. So it was that by May, 1847, the atmospheric system, on which half-a-million pounds had been squandered, was abandoned. This abandonment coincided with the amalgamation of the Croydon and Brighton lines to form the nucleus of the London Brighton & South Coast Railway.

Meantime there had been major developments to the south-west of London. As far back as 1831 there had been meetings in support of a proposal to link Southampton with London by rail, and a Bill authorising the construction of the London & Southampton Railway was passed in 1834. In 1835 a Bill was presented to authorise a branch from Basingstoke through Newbury, Devizes and Trowbridge to Bath and Bristol, but the Great Western Railway was also in the field with a Bill for a much more direct route to Bristol, which received Parliamentary sanction, whereas the London & Southampton branch did not. The latter company was fortunate in its engineer, Joseph Locke, who worked out a superbly aligned and graded route, particularly through the hilly chalk country to the south-west of Basingstoke, cutting like an arrow with its 16 miles of continuous 1 in 252 gradient from Litchfield through Winchester to Eastleigh. The year 1838 saw the opening of the main line from Waterloo to Woking; Basingstoke was reached by 1839; and the Basingstoke–Southampton section was complete by 1840. In 1839 the railway assumed the more comprehensive title of London & South Western Railway.

In retrospect it seems quite extraordinary that for half-a-century the LSWR took no notice of Bournemouth as a source of revenue. When the first extension westwards from Southampton took place, in 1847, it followed a very circuitous course —in part travelling south-east—to reach Brockenhurst, after which it made another wide circuit to the north through Ringwood before turning south to Wimborne and Broadstone and finally west to Wareham and Dorchester. So sinuous was the route that it became nicknamed "Castleman's Corkscrew" after its principal promoter. Not until 1870 was Bournemouth reached by a branch due south from Ringwood to Christchurch, brought into use in 1862, with an extension eight years later to what has now become one of the most popular seaside resorts in the entire country. All

▲ Early architectural extravagance—the northern entrance to Clayton tunnel on the London & Brighton line, with its cottage, still inhabited, between the two towers.　　　　　[D. T. Rowe

▲ The first locomotive of the first Southern constituent company—*Invicta* of the Canterbury & Whitstable Railway, built in 1830.　　　　[Loco. Publishing Co.

▼ Former South Eastern & Chatham 0-6-0 tank, with cut-down boiler mountings and cab for working through the limited clearance Tylers Hill tunnel on the Canterbury & Whitstable line, seen here.
　　　　　[P. Ransome-Wallis

NECTAR

these circuits, however, came to an end when in 1888 the present main line was opened direct from Brockenhurst to a new station at Bournemouth Central and on to Bournemouth West. Fourteen years earlier the latter had been opened as the terminus of the joint London & South Western and Midland Somerset & Dorset line, which as far as Poole now provided a direct route from Waterloo by the new Holes Bay spur to the Dorchester and Weymouth line.

As to the other main arms of the London & South Western Railway, Salisbury was reached from Basingstoke in 1857 and Exeter (Queen Street) three years later; 1862 saw the completion of the 1 in 37 descent from Exeter Queen Street into the Bristol & Exeter St. Davids station; this enabled the LSWR to link up with the Exeter & Crediton Railway, which it had taken over in 1854 from the B&ER, with the extension of the latter to Barnstaple. But the LSWR was destined to learn in later years, after its great competitor, the Great Western Railway, had absorbed the Bristol & Exeter in 1876, that the GWR at St. Davids could be unpleasantly obstructive at times to its rival's trains. The line from Yeoford Junction to Okehampton and Plymouth, completed in 1890, crossed Dartmoor by the highest summit on the Southern system, 950ft above sea level.

It was in 1859 that the London & South Western Railway completed its Portsmouth direct line through Guildford and Haslemere to Havant;

here it joined the coast line of the London Brighton & South Coast, which had made its way into Portsmouth 12 years earlier. Right up to the grouping the LSWR had to use the LBSCR line, by running powers, between Havant and the junctions at Farlington, but from there onwards the line into Portsmouth Town, together with the extension to Portsmouth Harbour, opened in 1876, was joint LSWR and LBSCR property. So also, across the Spithead, was Ryde Pier, which the two companies built, together with the pier railway and the Esplanade station, to link up with the Isle of Wight Railway at St. Johns Road. This was in 1880.

The Island railways had begun in 1862 with the short line from Cowes to Newport, followed two years later by the line from Ryde to Shanklin, and the extension through the St. Boniface Tunnel into Ventnor in 1866. This ultimately became the Isle of Wight Railway, but the later line from Newport to Ryde, with its branches from Newport to Ventnor Town and Merstone to Sandown, became the Isle of Wight Central. Then there was also the Freshwater, Yarmouth & Newport, which led a precarious existence at the western end of the Island. In the grouping all became a part of the Southern Railway. Few could have foreseen how after nationalisation all the railways in the Isle of Wight would disappear, save only the line from Ryde to Shanklin, and that this would be worked electrically by diminutive trains displaced from the London tubes.

◀ Cannon Street railway bridge over the Thames in SR days, with its total of ten running lines and sidings.   [British Railways

▼ Blackfriars bridge from the south, of the former London Chatham & Dover Railway, leading to Holborn Viaduct terminus.   [R. J. Marshall

2 · *Britain's First Large Scale Railway Amalgamation*

WE HAVE NOW to consider what had been happening in South-Eastern England during this period. Before many years had passed the South Eastern Railway was to learn that it was not to have an unchallenged monopoly of railway transport in the County of Kent, though for some time it was able to spread its wings without much interference. Branches were opened from Paddock Wood to Maidstone in 1844, from Ashford to Canterbury, Ramsgate and Margate in 1846, and from Tonbridge to Hastings between 1845 and 1852, while the former London & Greenwich Railway, which had reached Greenwich in 1838, by 1847 had been extended to Gravesend and Strood. This last, known as the North Kent Line, was carried through two tunnels, 1,530yd and 2,329yd in length, between Higham and Strood, which formerly had been occupied by the Thames & Medway Canal. At Strood the line terminated for a time, for to cross the Medway into Rochester and Chatham was regarded as too costly an undertaking.

The South Eastern Railway thus by the end of

▼ Hungerford bridge and Charing Cross terminus of the former South Eastern Railway, as it is seen to-day.
[J. H. Cooper-Smith

the 1840 decade had established a network of lines throughout Kent, though most of them were anything but direct. From London Bridge to Dover, for example, the distance via Redhill was 87 miles, while to Margate via Redhill and Ashford was no less than 102 miles, and by 1850 more direct railway communications were being seriously canvassed. As far back as 1824 and 1832 there had been schemes for lines through North Kent, and in 1838 a proposal for a railway from London by way of Gravesend and Rochester to Maidstone, from which one arm would proceed to Ashford, Folkestone and Dover, and the other to Canterbury and Sandwich.

But it was not until 1853 that Parliamentary powers were obtained for a modest independent line called the East Kent Railway, which would begin with an end-on junction with the SER North Kent branch at Strood and proceed through Chatham and Faversham to Canterbury. Even though this involved the use of the SER station at Strood, the latter's management did not oppose the plan, as it calculated on carrying to and from London through traffic which had not involved it in any constructional expense, especially that of bridging the Medway. But it was a different matter when, after having failed to obtain running powers over the SER from Strood into London, the East Kent in 1855 obtained the consent of Parliament for an extension from Canterbury to Dover, and in 1858, worse still, for further powers to build its own independent line from Strood to London. Both schemes were now vigorously opposed by the South Eastern, but to no effect.

The East Kent London extension powers envisaged a new line from Strood to Bromley, and from there a link to Shortlands, which by 1858 was reached by the West End of London & Crystal Palace Railway by way of a very ornate station at Crystal Palace Low Level. Running powers would be exercised over this line to Battersea and thence over the Victoria & Pimlico Railway across the Thames into the latter's Victoria Station. So it was that by 1860 it had become possible for East Kent trains to run through from Canterbury into the heart of London, and two years later from Dover also; by 1863 the East Kent, which in 1859 had assumed the more comprehensive title of London Chatham & Dover Railway, had completed its own independent line from Beckenham through the Penge Tunnel to Herne Hill and

10

Victoria. Also by 1863 the LCDR had completed a coast line from Faversham through Herne Bay to Margate and Ramsgate, providing a far shorter route from London to these resorts than that of its rival.

At this point it is interesting to recall what happened in the Medway area after the London Chatham & Dover had bridged the Medway and so connected Strood with Rochester and Chatham. A connection was laid in between the two lines on the Strood side of the river, but for years the antagonism between them was such that little use was made of it, and finally, in 1892, the South Eastern in desperation completed a new bridge across the Medway, parallel to that of the LCDR, and brought into operation a branch of its own to a terminus called Chatham Central. But after the fusion of the two railways in 1899, to which we shall come later, the South Eastern branch became redundant, and in 1911 it was closed down. In 1919 a fire on the former Chatham line's bridge caused a hasty restoration of the connection between the two lines, and the use once again of the South Eastern bridge for five months until the other bridge had been restored. So matters continued until 1927, when defects in the Chatham line bridge resulted in the decision to abandon it, and to divert all traffic to the newer South Eastern bridge, which is the one still in use.

Next the LCDR, not content with having crossed the Thames and obtained a West End terminal at Victoria, decided to penetrate the City as well, and in 1863 obtained powers for a line which would cross the river at Blackfriars, have a station within a quarter-of-a-mile of St. Paul's Cathedral at Ludgate Hill, and continue to join the Metropolitan Railway at Farringdon, so providing a direct link between the railways south and north of the Thames. The opening to Ludgate Hill took place at the end of 1864.

The threat thus posed by the new competitor to the South Eastern Railway was serious, and immediate steps to counter it had to be taken. It was necessary for the SER to obtain West End and City terminals similar to those of its rival, and Parliamentary powers were obtained in 1859 for an extension from London Bridge to Waterloo, where a connection would be made with the London & South Western terminus, and from there across the Thames to a West End terminus at Charing Cross.

It should be added here that the first proposals for a Charing Cross station had been made as far back as 1857, but it was the LCDR penetration to Victoria that forced the issue, and, moreover, the

▼ Grosvenor bridge of the one-time Victoria & Pimlico Railway, leading (far right) to Victoria station. [British Railways

building of a branch from London Bridge to yet a fourth crossing of the Thames into Cannon Street. Had the ultimate amalgamation taken place at an earlier date, it may be taken as certain that two City and two West End terminals, with four costly Thames bridges, would have been reduced in number. Charing Cross station was opened in 1864 and Cannon Street in 1866. The two lines separated close by Southwark Cathedral, at Borough Market Junction, destined in later years to become, as it still remains, an operating headache of the greatest severity.

The second threat to the South Eastern by its new competitor was that the latter's routes from London to Margate, Ramsgate and Dover were all shorter than those of the SER. They were much more steeply graded, however, with a saw-toothed profile of 1 in 100 inclines as far out as Rochester—including the formidable 5 miles of Sole Street bank westwards from Rochester Bridge —and with further 1 in 100 climbs to the Selling and Shepherdswell summits between Faversham and Dover. But curtailment of the South Eastern circuit through Redhill had now become imperative,

and in 1868 there was completed a new line direct from New Cross to Tonbridge by way of Chislehurst and Sevenoaks, which reduced the journey to points west of Tonbridge by 13 miles. This was done at the cost of some long and severe climbs from both directions to the summit at Knockholt, and of two tunnels, Polhill and Sevenoaks, the latter, 3,454yd in length, the longest on the Southern system.

In retrospect it seems astonishing that the South Eastern management, despite its heavy expenditure on the new London terminals and the direct New Cross–Tonbridge line, was not more concerned at the serious threat to its future posed by its rival. It had one substantial advantage, however, and that was the shaky financial position of the Chatham line. Indeed, in 1866 the latter, which until then had paid no dividends on its ordinary stock, was unable to meet its debenture interest, and Receivers in Chancery were appointed. The main contractors for the new LCDR construction,

▲ Waterloo station approach after the first electrification; with a Urie 4-6-2 tank starting a train of empty stock to Clapham Junction.   [P. Ransome-Wallis

who had largely financed it, and several banking houses, failed, and had it not been for the backing of the London & South Western and Great Northern Railways, who could see possibilities in future through traffic, it is difficult to know what might have happened to the insolvent railway company.

Now one of the Receivers was James Staats Forbes, formerly Manager of the Dutch Rhenish Railway, and who in 1862 had been appointed General Manager of the London Chatham & Dover. How the impecunious company could afford to pay him an annual salary of £1,500 (the same as that earned by the General Manager of the London & North Western!) and to offer him a 1 per cent commission if the net receipts after completion of the line to Dover exceeded those of the previous year, we may never know; but there it was. At first things went well under his management, but the growing demands of interest on the enormous capital sums that had been spent

finally brought about the 1866 crash. Nevertheless it was the Chairman of the company, Lord Sondes, who was forced to resign; there was no suggestion that Forbes should relinquish his office, and in 1873 he was appointed Chairman and Managing Director of the LCDR.

On the South Eastern side another figure of great note also had made his appearance, and it was Sir Edward Watkin, who was by way of being a successor to George Hudson, the former "Railway King". After experience on the London & North Western Railway, Watkin in 1854 had been appointed General Manager of the Manchester, Sheffield & Lincolnshire Railway. By 1865, having in the meantime secured his election as Member of Parliament for Hythe, he obtained a seat on the South Eastern Board, and just over a year later he had become Chairman. With his seats also on the Boards of the Great Eastern, Metropolitan and East London Railways, and with the 1899 extension to London which changed the MS&L to the Great Central Railway, Watkin had rosy dreams of a railway empire which would extend not merely from Lancashire to Folkestone

▲ Ryde Pier, built jointly by the London & South Western and London Brighton & South Coast Railways and opened in 1880. [British Railways

▼ Ryde Pier station, with the Southern Railway paddle-steamer *Sandown* from Portsmouth Harbour. [R. A. Panting

and Dover, but by the help of the projected Channel Tunnel to the Continent as well.

With two such dominant personalities as Forbes in the London Chatham & Dover chair and Watkin in that of the South Eastern there were bound to be clashes, and clashes there most certainly were—indeed, a bitter rivalry. With the lines of the two companies interlaced over much of Kent, there was every opportunity for fierce and at times wasteful competition, but at first the greatest competition was for the traffic to and from the Continent. In 1862 Forbes of the LCDR had obtained a considerable advantage by securing the mail contract from London to the Continent via Dover, which, oddly enough, had been offered to, but had been refused by, the SER. The reason was that as far back as 1843 the South Eastern management, with rare foresight, had bought up the then derelict Folkestone Harbour and had converted it into a cross-Channel port, with a shorter route from London to Paris via Boulogne than that via Dover–Calais. However, this particular competition came to an end when in 1865 a pooling arrangement for the Continental traffic was reached between the two companies, which turned out to be a good deal more to the advantage of the Chatham than of the South Eastern. Yet the competition still continued, with the Chatham penetrating into the heart of South Eastern territory in 1884 by a line from Maidstone to Ashford, and even trying in the same year, though unsuccessfully, to get Parliamentary sanction for a branch from Kearsney, on its Dover main line, into Folkestone.

At long last, as the century was drawing to its close, the competition came to an end. Sir Edward Watkin had given up his South Eastern Chairmanship in 1894, leaving Forbes in the field, but the reputation of both the SER and the LCDR with the public was anything but high. The Chairmanship of the SER had passed into able hands in the person of H. Cosmo Bonsor, and with Forbes on the verge of retirement also the decision was reached in 1898 for a fusion of the two companies under the title South Eastern & Chatham Railway Companies' Managing Committee. The net receipts were to be divided in the proportion of 59 per cent to the South Eastern and 41 per cent to the Chatham, which was only fair, seeing that SER shareholders had been drawing dividends up to $4\frac{1}{2}$ per cent, whereas the less fortunate holders of LCDR ordinary stock for years had had no return from their investment.

From the operating point of view the amalgamation offered great advantages, such as the cutting out of wasteful competition, the most economical use of interconnecting routes, and standardisation of locomotives and rolling stock. But so much had to be done to improve the financial position, especially on the Chatham side, that for the time being the unhappy South Eastern stockholders found their dividends reduced to $2\frac{1}{2}$ per cent, and not until 1910 had there been a recovery to $3\frac{1}{2}$ per cent, while those on the Chatham side got nothing at all until 1914. So the amalgamation, which became operative from January 1, 1899, began a new era in railway communication throughout the county of Kent.

▼ Ventnor terminus, Isle of Wight Railway, with its curious suggestion of cave dwellers below the cliff in the background.   [J. C. Beckett

▲ On the 1ft 11½in gauge Lynton & Barnstaple Railway
—2-6-2 tank No. 188 *Lew* and train.

[Loco. Publishing Co.

▼ The diminutive 2-6-2 tank *Lew* with train crossing
Chelfham viaduct on the 1ft 11½in gauge Lynton &
Barnstaple Railway.   [A. B. MacLeod

Little needs to be said about the development through these years of the London Brighton & South Coast system. It covered a triangle of territory with London at its apex, and Hastings and Portsmouth at its eastern and western extremities respectively. At the former it was in competition with the South Eastern Railway and at the latter with the London & South Western, but in neither case very effectively, so far as London traffic was concerned, because of its longer routes. To and from Brighton, Eastbourne, Worthing, Littlehampton and Bognor, however, it had a monopoly, with no invasion of its preserve by its neighbours, while at the same time it was developing a vast suburban traffic between its Victoria and London Bridge terminals and the South London suburbs. Its only intruder was the South Eastern line, opened in 1849, which from Redhill cut clean across both London Brighton & South Coast and London & South Western territory, through Dorking, Guildford and Aldershot, to link up with the Great Western Railway at Reading—a route which, if the Channel Tunnel should materialise, may well become one of the most important in the country.

By the time of the SER and LCDR amalgamation most of what was later to become the Southern Railway had come into existence, but one or two later additions are worth noting. One of the most interesting additions to the system was made in 1923, when the Southern took over the Lynton & Barnstaple Railway, which had been built privately and opened in 1898 to a gauge no wider than 1ft 11½in. Unhappily this unique example of Southern narrow gauge line went out of service in 1935. A branch which had a curiously chequered existence was that of the SECR from Nunhead to Crystal Palace High Level, which was closed in 1917, reopened in 1919, closed again between 1944 and 1946 and shut down finally under nationalisation in 1946.

In and about 1901 to 1905 the South Western became active in opening new branches, including Basingstoke–Alton–Fareham, Axminster–Lyme Regis, Budleigh Salterton–Exmouth, Bentley–Bordon and others, all of which have since vanished. But the Waterloo & City tube, irreverently known as the "Drain", has pursued a busy existence since its opening in 1898. The final merger of the South Eastern & Chatham, London Brighton & South Coast and London & South Western Railways took effect from January 1, 1923, with headquarters at Waterloo.

3 · *The Southern Takes Shape*

So January 1, 1923, saw the coming into existence of the Southern Railway. The Railways Act, 1921 laid it down that there would be five constituent companies—the London & South Western, London Brighton & South Coast, South Eastern and London Chatham & Dover Railways, and the South Eastern & Chatham Railway Companies' Managing Committee. From this it will be noted that up to the end of 1922 the LCDR and SER had still retained their separate identity, though controlled by the one Managing Committee. Further, the London & Greenwich and Mid-Kent Railways, with the Victoria Station & Pimlico Railway, which similarly up till now had continued to lead an independent existence (though for years past dependent on being operated by the SECR), were also absorbed by the Southern Railway. With them came in the three railways in the Isle of Wight, together with the North Cornwall; Plymouth, Devonport & South Western Junction; Lynton & Barnstaple; Totton & Fawley; Wimbledon & Sutton; and several smaller companies. The total extent of the new system was 2,178 route miles, or, including sidings, 5,381 miles of single track.

As to other statistics, the new group owned 2,281 locomotives, 7,500 passenger coaches and 36,749 wagons; the annual coaching mileage was 38,759,550 and freight mileage 6,359,418. The Southern Railway was destined to be the only one of the four groups whose receipts from passenger traffic would exceed those from the carriage of freight; but this was readily understandable because the SR provided access to more highly popular seaside resorts, right round the Kent, Sussex, Hampshire, Dorset, Devon and Cornwall coasts, than any other group, some of them also generating a thriving long-distance commuter traffic to and from London, not to mention the vast London suburban traffic, the flourishing

▼ Lewes station, London Brighton & South Coast Railway. Seaford branch train to right; "Schools" 4-4-0 on Victoria–Eastbourne express in centre; lines to Brighton to left.   [H. Thompson

▲ Crystal Palace Low Level station of the former London Brighton & South Coast Railway. [R. C. Riley

cross-Channel Continental traffic, and the service of the port of Southampton. For its maritime activities the Southern had come into possession of 41 steamships and a total quayage in docks and wharves extending to all but 11 miles.

Who was to direct the fortunes of the new company? A trial was made at first of a joint General Managership, in which the General Managers of the SECR, LBSCR and LSWR—Sir Percy Tempest, Sir William Forbes and Sir Herbert Walker respectively—all shared. But such a proposition was soon proved wholly impractical, and the final choice fell on Sir Herbert Walker, who had come from the London & North Western Railway to the London & South Western as General Manager in 1912, and was known to have considerable ability; he succeeded to the managerial chair on January 1, 1924. As subsequent events proved, no finer choice could have been made. In the early stages of the 1914–1918 war Walker so distinguished himself that as early as 1915 he had earned, not merely a knighthood, but a KCB. Another highly successful choice was that of R. E. L. Maunsell, Chief Mechanical Engineer of the SECR, to occupy the same position in the SR establishment.

An early threat to the new company was the proposal of the City & South London Railway to extend its tube from Clapham Common to Morden, and from there to a junction at Wimbledon with the East Putney & Wimbledon line of the former LSWR (used by the Metropolitan District Railway into Wimbledon), from which a new line would be carried on to a terminus alongside Sutton SR station. Needless to say, the Southern opposed this prospective invasion of its territory. Finally, the City & South London powers were curtailed to Morden, to which the CSLR opened in 1926; the Wimbledon & Sutton Railway was promoted as a separate company, and opened in 1930, but worked from the start by the Southern, and, as already mentioned, absorbed by the Southern at the grouping.

Soon after Sir Herbert Walker had taken office as General Manager, the Southern Railway began to attract some very invidious attention from the national press. For this there were reasons. Electrification was proceeding apace, and this meant permanent way restrictions, and a shortage of suburban stock, due to the number of coaches temporarily withdrawn for conversion to electric working. New timetables introduced in 1924 in order as far as possible to co-ordinate the working between the three divisions had caused a good deal of dissatisfaction. As a result, overcrowding was rife, and punctuality had fallen to a low ebb. At this stage Sir Herbert had a stroke of genius. It was to attract from the ranks of the enemies in the newspaper world a man of ability who would be prepared to come to the defence of the railway. This proved to be John Blumenfeld Elliot, son of the Editor of the *Daily Express*, who himself had had experience as Assistant Editor of the *Evening Standard*.

So to Waterloo John Elliot came, to establish a new Public Relations Department, which he did with brilliant success. Large advertisements were inserted in the daily papers, explaining the difficulties with which the railway was having temporarily to cope, and what it had been doing to recover from the arrears of maintenance and other handicaps caused by the late war. The impression made on the public was such that the criticisms soon died down, and in the succeeding years the great benefits of Southern electrification and other large-scale improvements soon proved that the forecast of better times had been fully justified. As for John Elliot, a man of such genius was not to be confined for long to the mere matter of publicity; in course of time he himself was destined to succeed to the position of General Manager of the Southern Railway, later still to the even more important post of General Manager of the London Midland & Scottish Railway, and eventually to a knighthood.

So the Southern Railway was established on a firm footing. Later chapters describe some of the principal happenings during the quarter of a century of its history, together with those of its constituent companies that made possible its notable development.

▲ The imposing entrance to the new Waterloo terminus of the London & South Western Railway on its opening day, March 21, 1922, with its "Victory" arch. [British Railways

4 · The Way and Works

WHILE the Southern Railway has never boasted any major engineering works comparable, say, to the Forth Bridge or the Severn Tunnel, the laying of some of the main lines of its constituent companies involved engineering work of a high order. Mention has been made already of the way in which Joseph Locke carried his London & Southampton line with arrow straightness and a perfectly even 1 in 252 gradient through the chalk hills of Hampshire past Winchester by means of tunnels, deep cuttings and high embankments—an outstanding example of railway location work. Cubitt of the South Eastern was responsible for 46 miles of all but dead straight line between Redhill and Ashford, but through much easier country. Similarly Rastrick did fine work in carrying the London & Brighton main line through from Croydon to Brighton with nothing steeper than his sweeping 1 in 264 ups-and-downs, and with no more costly engineering works than his Merstham, Balcombe and Clayton Tunnels, and the fine viaduct across the Ouse Valley just north of Haywards Heath, though he could do nothing, of course, about the already existing 1 in 100 climb of the London & Croydon Forest Hill bank.

Another section which called for engineering skill of a high order was the South Eastern main line between Folkestone and Dover. When Cubitt had brought his line down on an even 1 in 264 gradient from the high ground at Westenhanger into Folkestone he was still at a considerable level above the sea, and needed a viaduct 100ft in height over the lower part of the town before he could continue eastwards. Next, beyond the short Martello Tunnel, he entered the wild strip of coastline between the chalk cliffs and the sea that is known as the Warren. Two headlands lay in front of him—Abbott's Cliff and Shakespeare's Cliff—and between them a smaller promontory known as the Round Down Cliff. The chalk of which the two former were composed seemed

▼ The handsome viaduct across Brighton carrying the Lewes line from London Road station (foreground) into Brighton Central.　　　　　　[J. A. M. Vaughan

reasonably sound, but not the Round Down. Cubitt therefore decided on the bold idea of dynamiting the Round Cliff out of his way, and this with Army assistance was carried out successfully. When he reached Shakespeare's Cliff, as there were some slight doubts about the soundness of its chalk, Cubitt drove two single line tunnels, each in the shape of a Gothic arch, for greater safety, which accounts for the unusual appearance of their entrances.

So the difficult work of this final 7 miles was carried to completion, but it could little have been foreseen what trouble might ensue in later years because of the unstable nature of the chalk cliffs that more or less overhung the line. General Pasley, who conducted the Board of Trade inspection before the opening of the line in 1844, did not consider that this constituted any risk, but he was wrong. After stable conditions had continued for more than thirty years, there came a very serious slip in 1877 at the east end of the Martello Tunnel, extending over about a hundred acres, and closing the line for some time. Other slips of lesser extent occurred in 1881, 1885, 1886, 1892 and 1896, but by far the worst was yet to come.

During the month of December 1915 there had been an abnormal rainfall in East Kent, and a slight slip of the chalk between the Martello and Abbott's Cliff Tunnels had resulted in the stationing of a watchman in the Warren as a precautionary measure. On the evening of December 19, just as a train was leaving Folkestone Junction for Dover, he heard the first sounds of a much bigger movement, but though it was now dark he succeeded in alerting the train's driver just as the train was emerging from Martello Tunnel and getting the train brought to a stand. This was the beginning of a cliff fall and landslide on an immense scale, which extended over nearly two miles and at the maximum pushed the track some 160ft out of line.

As this was in the early stages of the 1914–1918 war, with the Government in control of the railways, no mention of what had happened got into the newspapers. Also because of war conditions it was impossible to spare sufficient labour to make restoration of the line possible. Indeed, there was some talk of abandoning it altogether, after the experiences of the last 38 years, and of relying thenceforward on the Chatham line to Dover, to which all traffic had been diverted.

▲ On the former LSWR Plymouth main line—the Tavy viaduct, near Bere Ferrers.   [R. E. Vincent

After the war, however, it was realised that the South Eastern route to Dover was too valuable to lose, and the mammoth task was taken in hand of removing 82,000,000cu yd of chalk and soil before the track could be put in running order once again. Not until August 1, 1919, after an interruption of 3¾ years, and an expenditure of £310,000, was communication restored between Folkestone and Dover. It may be added that the immured train, which had been twisted into a corkscrew shape by the landslip, was eventually rescued by being drawn back vehicle by vehicle through the Martello Tunnel by hawsers.

Mention of tunnels brings its reminder that by far the majority of the longest on the Southern Railway were to be found on its South Eastern & Chatham lines. Sevenoaks, 1 mile 1,693yd, headed the list, and had as its neighbour on the SER main line to Dover, Polhill Tunnel, 1 mile 851yd. Abbott's Cliff Tunnel, already mentioned, was 1 mile 182yd in length, and the approach of the Chatham line to Dover was through the Lydden Tunnel, 1 mile 609yd. Strood Tunnel, which as mentioned earlier once housed the Thames & Medway Canal, was 1 mile 569yd long. On the original SER main line to Tonbridge via Redhill there was Merstham Tunnel, 1 mile 71yd, which had to be bored through the North Downs, and when the London Brighton & South Coast Railway built its independent Redhill avoiding line between Coulsdon and Earlswood, Merstham was supplemented by the parallel Quarry Tunnel, 1 mile 353yd. Further south the Brighton main line had to penetrate the South Downs by Clayton Tunnel, 1 mile 499yd. The list of Southern tunnels exceeding one mile in length was completed by

Penge Tunnel, 1 mile 381yd, on the former Chatham main line. There were no tunnels a mile or more long on the former London & South Western Railway.

But the LSWR could certainly claim the most spectacular viaduct on the Southern system, the lattice steel Meldon Viaduct, 150ft in height at its maximum, across the West Okement Valley just short of the point where the Exeter to Plymouth main line reached the highest altitude on the Southern system, 950ft above the sea. In complete contrast with spidery Meldon structure were the massive bridges which the Southern constituent railways threw across the River Thames to reach their London terminals. These were the Cannon Street Bridge and the Hungerford Bridge into Charing Cross of the South Eastern Railway; and the Blackfriars Bridge of the London Chatham & Dover Metropolitan Extension and the latter's share of the Grosvenor Bridge (built originally by the Victoria Station & Pimlico Railway) giving access to Victoria, with the other half shared by the London Brighton & South Coast Railway. Both these railways joined forces in widening the Grosvenor Bridge in 1866 at a cost of £161,000.

All these were and still are bridges of considerable size, each carrying a number of running lines and sidings. Today the Grosvenor Bridge, which in recent years has been completely rebuilt, carries 10 tracks; Hungerford Bridge accommodates 6 lines and Cannon Street Bridge 8 (formerly 10); while Blackfriars Bridge bears 8 tracks and at its northern side the outer end of Blackfriars passenger station. Cannon Street Bridge may be taken as an example of the scale of these structures; it has two side spans of 131ft each and three middle spans of 148ft, with a total width of bridge floor of 66ft 8in. It is carried on cast-iron columns of 18ft diameter

<table>
<tr><td>

▲ The Hayling Island branch of the LBSCR crossing Langstone Harbour. Note the diminutive size of the "Terrier" 0-6-0 tank with its train.   [P. H. Townend

</td><td>

▼ The western end of Shakespeares Cliff tunnel, on the main London–Dover line, with "Schools" 4-4-0 No. 911 *Dover* emerging. Note the unusual pointed arch of the portal.   [Timothy H. Cobb

</td></tr>
</table>

▼ The unstable wilderness of Folkestone Warren, which has given serious trouble with landslips. The modern "Golden Arrow" is seen travelling towards Folkestone.   [J. H. Cooper-Smith

below the water level and 12ft above. It cost £193,000, and its neighbour at Charing Cross, with its six 154ft spans, £180,000.

It may be added that the Metropolitan Extension to Blackfriars involved the building of a viaduct 5¾ miles long, with 742 brick arches and 94 girder spans. On the Brighton main line the Ouse Valley viaduct has been mentioned already; this notable masonry structure, 90ft high at the maximum, has thirty-seven 30ft arches in its length of 1,440ft.

Although the London & South Western Railway was not involved in any Thames crossing to reach its terminus at Waterloo, it had to bridge the river at a number of points upstream. These were at Putney Bridge, Kew Bridge, Barnes, Richmond, Kingston, Staines and Windsor, making a total of eleven Thames bridges that were inherited by the Southern Railway after the grouping. The biggest of the LSWR contributions was Putney Bridge, on their former Wimbledon & Fulham line, with five 143ft and three 90ft spans.

A word is now necessary about the gradients of the principal lines. We have already seen how by most able planning Locke, Rastrick and Cubitt engineered their respective London & Southampton, London & Brighton and South Eastern main lines with astonishing straightness and ruling gradients which throughout were no steeper than 1 in 250 to 1 in 264. But it was a different matter with many of the later lines. The direct South Eastern line from New Cross to Tonbridge introduced gradients as steep as 1 in 120 up to Elmstead Woods and Knockholt, and 6 miles continuously down at 1 in 144–122 from Sevenoaks to Tonbridge. The London Chatham & Dover main line almost throughout its length to Dover was plagued with long 1 in 100 inclines, up to and including the 5 miles of Sole Street bank. From Effingham up to Wadhurst on the SER Hastings branch was a 7-mile bank at 1 in 97 to 132, and the Maidstone–Ashford line had a climb out of Maidstone as steep as 1 in 60.

West of Salisbury on the main line to Plymouth the gradients became progressively steeper until they reached the 6 miles at 1 in 80 up to Honiton Tunnel, but that was little in comparison with the ascent from Exeter to the 950ft summit beyond Okehampton, with 22 miles of almost uninterrupted climbing from Crediton, 15 miles of it at 1 in 76–77. Not far away, in the same county of Devon, was the Ilfracombe branch, with its 3 miles at 1 in 40 up to Mortehoe and its near-precipitous 2¼ miles at 1 in 36 down into Ilfracombe, and the terminus still at a considerable height above the town and the sea. Unhappily both these lines have now disappeared under the axe of rationalisation. So also has the Canterbury & Whitstable line, with its short 1 in 28, but this is nearly approached by another steep pitch on a line that is still of considerable importance—the ¾-mile down at 1 in 30 by which the Dover main line at Folkestone Junction is connected with Folkestone Harbour.

▼ Deep down in Merstham chalk cutting on the LBSCR Quarry line—a Brighton–Victoria express headed by "King Arthur" 4-6-0 No. 796, *Sir Dodinas le Savage*.   [E. R. Wethersett

▲ A junction layout of note—Worting, near Basingstoke, where the Southampton and Bournemouth
trains can divert from or join the straight Salisbury
line at speeds up to 60 mph.   [British Railways

▼ The Hampton Court Junction flyover, with the down
Hampton Court line carried over the main lines by a
skew span of 155ft, and just beyond the bridge the
divergence to Cobham is seen.

5 · Southern Stations

In its London terminus at Waterloo the Southern Railway could claim to possess the largest and finest railway station in Great Britain. Today this claim may be challenged by the London Midland Region's Euston terminus, but that is as the result of a far more recent reconstruction. The two cases are very similar, for both stations, before their rebuilding, were an awkward collection of separate units which had been added in stages before they became welded into one comprehensive and well-arranged whole. Actually it was the constituent London & South Western Railway which was responsible for the 12-year task of transforming Waterloo, brought to a triumphant conclusion with the opening of the new station by Her Majesty Queen Mary on March 21, 1922, just over nine months before the LSWR lost its identity in the newly-formed Southern Railway.

The first Waterloo, opened in 1848 after extension by the London & South Western from its original Nine Elms terminus, was a modest structure with three platforms and four approach lines, which it was considered at the time "would be amply sufficient for present and future needs". In 1862 platforms were added for Windsor line trains, and in 1879 a separate South Station was opened to house the suburban trains to and from the Epsom, Hampton Court and other branches. The year 1885 saw the addition of another separate section, the North Station, for the Windsor line trains.

By now the number of platforms had grown to 18, but far from conveniently arranged, with the South Station as a kind of annexe reached by a covered bridge, and separated from the North Station by the Central Station, which handled the main line traffic. Incidentally, one line of the latter was extended by a bridge across the Waterloo Road to join the South Eastern Railway in their adjacent Waterloo Junction, and this connection for a time was used by through London & North Western trains which worked from Euston to Cannon Street by way of the West London line; later the connection served from time to time for exchanging vehicles between the two companies and for occasional Royal specials.

Towards the end of the last century it was realised that nothing short of a complete reconstruction would solve the Waterloo problem, and Parliamentary powers for the work were obtained in 1899 and 1900. Not until 1910, however, had the South Station been replaced by six new platforms, reached from a spacious circulating area. The Central Station rebuilding proved a more difficult task, but eventually nine similar plat-

▼ Cannon Street terminus just before the abolition of steam workings to the coast. "Schools" class 4-4-0 No. 30920 *Rugby* at the head of an evening commuter express to Hastings.   [R. C. Riley]

forms, with a central carriageway and an extension of the circulating area, were married to the North Station, which because of its more recent construction it was arranged to leave without much alteration. The main feature of the new Waterloo was the wide concourse, extending in a curve over the entire width of the station from Platform 1 to Platform 21, and flanked by the fine range of office buildings which were to become the headquarters of the Southern Railway. The frontage of the office building was completed by the magnificent "Victory Arch" which forms the main entrance.

The future length to which trains might grow was not entirely foreseen; only No. 11 platform was as long as 860ft and Nos. 12 to 14 from 828 to 838ft. The result has been that 12 coaches of modern stock are the maximum length of train that Waterloo station can accommodate today, though with later platform lengthening this now applies to platforms 7 to 14 inclusive. By the time of the reconstruction the number of approach tracks had increased from four to eight. The rail entrance to the station was controlled by "A" signalbox, which spanned all tracks, and was crowned by a spectacular array of semaphore arms which at one period reached the formidable total of 67, manually operated by 266 levers. The number of the latter would have been even greater but for the installation of a number of "gear" levers, each

▼ Charing Cross terminus after the roof rebuilding which followed the disastrous roof collapse in 1905.
[R. C. Riley

of which could be made to operate up to three signal arms. But by the completion of the station reconstruction route-indicating signals were beginning to come into use, and during the life of the Southern Railway electric colour-light signals replaced the old semaphores, and the "A" box gantry was swept away and replaced by a new all-electric box on the up side of the approach lines.

Next in scale among the London terminals of the Southern Railway was Victoria. This formerly was two stations side by side, the London, Brighton & South Coast terminus which was opened in 1860, and that of the London Chatham & Dover Railway, brought into use two years later. The Brighton station was actually built by the independent Victoria Station & Pimlico Railway, but from its opening was leased to the LBSCR. In precisely the same year, 1899, that the London & South Western Railway was obtaining Parliamentary powers for the complete reconstruction of Waterloo, the Brighton line sought and obtained similar powers to rebuild and extend its Victoria terminus. But whereas the LSWR was able to acquire all the land needed for lateral extension, the LBSCR, bounded on one side by the former LCDR and now SECR terminus, and on the other by Buckingham Palace Road, could only extend longitudinally, so producing a terminal station which in its arrangement has no parallel in Great Britain.

The old station had eight platforms, in two pairs separated by a wide carriage road, extending as far

▼ A striking view in modern days of the approach to Waterloo, taken from the adjacent multi-storey Shell building. [J. H. Cooper-Smith

▲ The spacious concourse at Waterloo after the opening of the enlarged terminus in 1922. [British Railways

as the Eccleston Bridge. In the new station a spacious circulating area led to seven platforms, bounded on the west side by a new carriage road; then adjacent to Buckingham Palace Road were two more platforms, Nos. 8 and 9, shorter at their inner ends but extending beyond Eccleston Bridge as far as Elizabeth Bridge. So also did the new Nos. 1 to 7, but with this difference, that beyond Eccleston Bridge a third track was laid in between each pair of platforms, allowing for exit from and entrance to the inner end of each of these platforms when trains were standing at their outer ends. In effect, therefore, this arrangement doubled platforms 2 to 7 inclusive, increasing the total number of platforms to 15. It cannot be said that the travelling public has greatly appreciated leaving or joining trains at the outer or north ends of the extended platforms, as this has involved them in a walk not far short of a quarter-of-a-mile to and from the ticket barriers; though more immediate access has been possible by stairways from Eccleston Bridge. Actually, however, these extensions have had and still do have no more than limited use.

The reconstruction lengthened the platforms concerned from 600ft to 1,500ft; the area covered by the station increased from 230ft by 800ft to 320ft by 1,500ft, and from $8\frac{1}{2}$ to 16 acres. After the formation of the Southern Railway, the two sides of Victoria became amalgamated as a single station not far short of Waterloo in area. The South Eastern & Chatham side contributed a further eight platforms, bringing the total up to 17,

which from then on were numbered consecutively from No. 1 on the SECR side to No. 17 adjoining Buckingham Palace Road on the LBSCR side. With the extensions of what had been Nos. 10 to 15 inclusive added, the effective total of platforms increased to 23, making this from the operating point of view the largest terminal station in Great Britain. One function of major importance exercised by the SECR side of Victoria throughout Southern Railway history has been the handling of all cross-Channel Continental traffic via Dover and Folkestone, with the Newhaven–Dieppe trains, formerly LBSCR, still dealt with on the adjacent Brighton side. Special facilities have always been provided on the SECR side for the reception of foreign Royalties and other eminent persons who have been brought to London by the Southern after crossing the Channel, latterly from Gatwick Airport more than the Channel Ports. Invariably this special traffic is handled at Platform No. 2.

At no stage of its history, even up to the present day, could any encomiums be awarded to the other London Brighton & South Coast terminus. Actually the first London Bridge was the earliest railway station to be opened in the heart of London, in December 1836, as the terminus of the London & Greenwich Railway; in 1839 the London & Croydon Railway began to use the London & Greenwich tracks into an adjacent London Bridge station of its own. After the former had become leased to the South Eastern Railway in 1845, there came the extension of the SER from London Bridge to Charing Cross, opened in 1864, followed in 1866 by the branch from the latter into Cannon Street; from then onwards the South Eastern trains were dealt with at a new High Level station at London Bridge, eventually enlarged to seven tracks with six platform faces. The four Low Level terminal platforms of the London & Greenwich were still retained by the SER, however, while the London Brighton & South Coast station finally expanded to eleven platforms. As at Victoria, after the formation of the Southern Railway the entire station was reorganised as one whole, with the platforms, 21 in all, renumbered consecutively from the SECR to the Brighton side. The last platform was and is No. 22, because No. 5 track has no platform.

That the South Eastern Railway went to the expense of adding Cannon Street to its Charing Cross terminus was due to the fact that its fierce rival, the London Chatham & Dover Railway, was penetrating into the heart of the City with its new line to Ludgate Hill, completed in 1864 and 1865, and extended further to Holborn Viaduct in 1874. The importance of this connection was increased when at the beginning of 1866 an extension was opened which dived down to join the Metropolitan Circle line with a triangular junction at Farringdon; in later years this was to be extensively used by passenger trains between Moorgate and SECR stations and also between the latter and suburban stations of the Great Northern Railway. For many years this was also the principal freight route between the Great Northern and Midland lines and SECR marshalling yards in South London.

<A Exeter Queen Street station (now Exeter Central) of the former London & South Western Railway.
[G. Freeman Allen

Ludgate Hill was anything but a pretentious station; indeed there were many public complaints about its two island platforms, which with a width no greater than 17ft could be even dangerous if crowded; but in 1910 there was a reconstruction which substituted a single island, 32ft wide, with the main lines to and from Holborn Viaduct carried alongside without platforms. From then on the only trains calling at Ludgate Hill were those to and from the Metropolitan line, but this was no hardship to passengers, as Holborn Viaduct was only 17ch away to the north, and St. Paul's, opened in 1886, was even closer, at a distance of 8ch. In these circumstances it was no surprise when in 1929 the Southern Railway closed Ludgate Hill station. St. Paul's, the present Blackfriars, was and still is partly a terminus, with four terminal platforms, but these are in use only in the peak morning and evening hours, to supplement the limited four-platform accommodation at Holborn Viaduct, just over ¼-mile away.

Finally we have Charing Cross and Cannon Street, which stand on land of such high value that any possibility of extension has been ruled out. The Charing Cross site measures 680ft by 170ft, and accommodates six platforms; that at Cannon Street, 855ft by 205ft, provides space for eight platforms. At one time the approach to Cannon Street, like that to Waterloo, was spanned by a gantry carrying the signalbox, with 243 levers; this was removed when in 1926 the Southern Railway carried out a reconstruction of the entire layout, a task which made it necessary to close the station completely for 22 days. The original layout had been planned to facilitate the working of Charing Cross trains into and out of Cannon Street, before they reached London Bridge, involving reversal at Cannon Street, but this practice had ceased, and the new layout was to simplify the operating.

December 5, 1905, witnessed a remarkable accident at Charing Cross. Without warning, one of the tie-rods of the all-over station roof suddenly failed, causing the collapse of two bays of the roof and of the large wind screen at the outer end of the station; this collapse in its turn caused the adjacent part of the station wall to fall outwards and crash on to the wall and roof of the Avenue Theatre. Had this occurred during the evening peak hour the results might have been terrible; but it was in mid-afternoon, and miraculously the only casualties were three railway employees, two of whom were at work on the roof, which at that time was 42 years old. Not until March 19, 1906, was it possible to reopen the station, after it had been completely re-roofed.

If we sum up the platform accommodation at these seven Southern Railway terminal stations in London—Victoria with its 23 platforms, Waterloo and London Bridge with 21 each, Cannon Street 8, Charing Cross 6 and Holborn Viaduct and Blackfriars 4 apiece—we have the almost unbelievable total of 87 platforms. Moreover, to give access to these stations has required 8 running lines into and out of Waterloo, 11 to and from London Bridge, contracting on the SE&C side to 6 over Cannon Street bridge and 4 at the approach to Charing Cross, with finally 4 into and out of Blackfriars. Almost all this trackage was in

▲ A handsome reconstruction in Southern Railway days: the exterior of Horsham station on the mid-Sussex line.   [British Railways

▼ Final Southern style in station building—Chessington North with its reinforced platform awnings.   [British Railways

existence before electrification began in 1909, but electric working, by attracting more and more residents to the suburbs round south-west, south and south-east London, not to mention the districts as far further out as the Channel coast resorts, has been the principal factor in building up an enormous commuter demand, which to-day taxes both the stations and their approach lines to the extreme limit.

Considerations of space prevent any detailed description of many fine provincial stations on the Southern system, a number of them rebuilt and enlarged during the 25 years of Southern Railway history. Most of the seaside resorts have been provided with commodious new stations, such as Ramsgate, opened in 1926, which with a new connecting line replaced the former Ramsgate Harbour (LCDR) and Ramsgate Town (SER) stations; Hastings (1931); and Southampton West, renamed Southampton Central after its reconstruction in 1935, with several others. Nearer London handsome stations have been provided at Wimbledon, Surbiton, Horsham and various other places, all with the attractive and distinctive features that have characterised modern Southern Railway architecture.

6 · *Pre-Grouping Southern Locomotives*

THE LOCOMOTIVES brought into the Southern Railway fold at the time of the grouping were about as varied an assortment of types and classes as they well could be. Some of the Locomotive Superintendents of the constituent companies had been men of considerable individuality, and there were features of their designs which had no parallels on other British railways. This was particularly the case with the dour Dugald Drummond, who controlled the fortunes of the London & South Western Locomotive Department from 1895 until his sudden death in 1912. It was during his reign, in 1909, that LSWR locomotive building was transferred from its cramped location at Nine Elms in South London to far more spacious conditions at Eastleigh, near Southampton.

Drummond had been preceded by William Adams, who will be chiefly remembered for his graceful outside-cylinder 4-4-0 express engines, a design which actually had originated with the latter's predecessor, W. G. Beattie, in 1876. This design had caused a mild sensation on its appearance, as until then passenger engines with leading bogies were rare. It had a distinctive appearance, with a long flat-topped splasher over the coupled wheels that gave these 20 locomotives the appearance of side tank engines. Various developments of this 4-4-0 design followed until we come to the handsome series of 60 4-4-0s which began to emerge from Nine Elms in 1890, Classes X2 and T6 with 7ft 1in coupled wheels, and Classes T3 and X6, intended for work west of Salisbury, with 6ft 7in wheels. With the flowing lines of their brass-beaded splashers and their tapered stovepipe

▼ LSWR Beattie 4-4-0 No. 364 (Class 348, 1876).
[Loco. Publishing Co.

chimneys, these Adams 4-4-0s presented a very attractive appearance. Outside cylinders and stovepipe chimneys were a standard feature of Adams designs, and he even went as far in 1893 as to design an 8ft 4-2-2 on these lines, but this was never built.

The advent of Dugald Drummond in 1895 resulted in an almost immediate reversal of many Adams principles. Outside cylinders for the time being were banished; chimneys with flared tops began to replace the stovepipes; safety-valves were transferred from the fireboxes to the locomotives' domes. Another characteristic Drummond feature which soon began to appear on his passenger tender engines was cross-water-tubes in their fireboxes, easily recognisable by the large patch on their firebox sides between the coupled wheel splashers. The idea was to improve firebox circulation, but it was never copied by any other locomotive engineer.

Drummond's third design was unique. It was a "double single", with two inside cylinders driving the leading pair of driving wheels, and two outside cylinders the rear pair, and without these wheels being coupled. For his four-cylinder arrangement he had, of course, to overcome his reluctance to use outside cylinders. But the boiler of No. 720 proved inadequate to supply four cylinders as large as $16\frac{1}{2}$in × 26in, and five later engines of the same type had 14in × 26in cylinders only. No. 720 in 1905 received a larger boiler, and a reduction in cylinder diameter to 14in. These 4-2-2-0s had a good turn of speed, but never greatly distinguished themselves.

Not so, however, with Drummond's T9 Class 4-4-0s, of which between 1899 and 1901 no fewer

than 66 took the road. Of these one unusual feature was their 10ft coupled wheelbase, the longest in the country at that time. They had $18\frac{1}{2}$in × 26in cylinders, 6ft 7in coupled wheels, 24sq ft firegrate area and 175lb pressure. Eventually all these engines were equipped with the characteristic Drummond bogie tenders, with inside bearings, which had first appeared with the 4-2-2-0s, and whose 4,000gal capacity was made necessary by the absence of water-troughs on the LSWR system. The "Greyhounds", as the T9s became nicknamed, with little doubt were Drummond's most successful design. For myself I have a vivid recollection of my first ride on the footplate of one of them, No. 113, which whisked the 15.30 out of Waterloo from Salisbury to Exeter, 88.0 miles of difficult gradients, in 94min 40sec, reaching $77\frac{1}{2}$ mph at Gillingham, $80\frac{1}{2}$ at Sherborne and Axminster and $86\frac{1}{2}$ at Broad Clyst, with an eight-coach train of 240 tons. I never timed anything as fast with a Drummond 4-6-0.

In 1903 Drummond produced a larger version of his T9 4-4-0, the S11 class, of which 10 were built, but with 6ft coupled wheels only, for service over the heavy grades between Salisbury and Exeter; and these were followed by the similar large-boilered L12s, 20 in number, with 6ft 7in wheels, which were allocated mainly to the Bournemouth service. But Drummond was hankering after something more powerful, and his thoughts were now turning towards the 4-6-0 wheel arrangement, in conjunction with four cylinders. So, in 1905, there appeared No. 330, first of a series of 4-6-0s which by current standards seemed simply immense machines. Nos. 330 to 334, Class F13, had four 16in × 24in cylinders,

6ft coupled wheels, 5ft 6in boilers pitched with centres 9ft above rail, 2,727sq ft heating surface, 31.5sq ft grate area and 175lb pressure. In 1907 No. 335 followed, with four $16\frac{1}{2}$in × 26in cylinders.

Then came Nos. 448–457, of Classes E3, G14 and P14, with smaller boilers, built between 1908 and 1911, and in Drummond's final year, 1912, the T14s, with 6ft 7in coupled wheels and boilers carrying 200lb pressure and pitched up to 9ft $3\frac{1}{2}$in above rail. None of the Drummond 4-6-0s, 26 in all, could be regarded as an outstanding success in its original form, and not until Urie and Maunsell had improved them in later years, particularly with superheating, did some of them justify their massive dimensions. The single long splasher over the coupled wheels earned the T14s the nickname of "Paddleboxes". The 4-6-0s were Drummond's first engines to carry their safety-valves over their fireboxes instead of above their domes.

Drummond died while his last express engines, the D15 class, were under construction. These handsome and competent machines, 10 in number, were the final development of his L12 4-4-0 design, but now with $19\frac{1}{2}$in × 26in cylinders, 6ft 7in coupled wheels, 27sq ft firegrate area, and 200lb pressure. Among their equipment were smokebox superheaters, feed-water heating apparatus, and, needless to say, cross water-tubes in their fireboxes. Among the innovations for which Drummond was responsible during his reign was the steam-driven motorcar, of which his No. 1, turned out in 1903, was the first of its kind in the country. Fifteen in all were built, and were followed by 12 diminutive 0-4-0 tanks for local push-and-pull services.

It was during Drummond's term of office that the title of Locomotive Superintendent was changed to Chief Mechanical Engineer, and it was to this

▼ LSWR Adams 4-4-0 No. 678 (Class T6, 1895).
[Loco. Publishing Co.

▲ LSWR Drummond 4-2-2-0 No. 371 with water-tube firebox and bogie tender on up Exeter express.
[F. E. Mackay

▼ LSWR Drummond 4-4-0 No. 312 (Class T9, 1901).
[Loco. Publishing Co.

that Robert Wallace Urie succeeded in 1912. Once again the new broom was destined to sweep very clean. Very soon the Drummond cross water-tubes in the firebox, smokebox steam-driers, stovepipe chimneys, and inside frames for tender bogies had been discarded, also four-cylinder propulsion for 4-6-0 locomotives. Urie's first design was a straightforward two-cylinder mixed traffic 4-6-0 with 21in × 28in cylinders, 6ft coupled wheels, 30sq ft firegrate area and 180lb pressure; while No. 490 used saturated steam, the remainder of this Class H15 were the first LSWR engines to be superheated, a Urie type of super-heater being adopted after trials with the Schmidt and Robinson types. It was from this beginning that Urie developed the Class N15 4-6-0s, 20 of which were built between 1918 and 1923, and which later, as modified by Maunsell, were to form part of the famous "King Arthur" class to which further reference is made in the next chapter. At first the N15s had cylinders of an unusual size— 22in × 28in—but these were soon lined up to 21in diameter. A mixed traffic version of the N15 class was the S15s, with coupled wheels of 5ft 7in diameter only, and lower-pitched boilers. Of these 20 in all were built during 1920 and 1921.

Urie will also be remembered for the four massive 4-8-0 tanks (Class G16) that he built to work the hump marshalling yard at Feltham, and the equally massive five 4-6-2 tanks (Class H16) for operating the exchange freight traffic between Feltham and the sidings of the London & North Western Railway at Willesden and the Midland Railway at Brent. In all, at the grouping Urie handed over the locomotive stock of the London & South Western Railway in an appreciably more competent condition than that in which he had taken it over eleven years earlier, but he had not learned the lessons of increased thermal efficiency that were to be applied by his Southern Railway successor, R. E. L. Maunsell.

We come now to the London Brighton & South Coast Railway, with the early locomotive history of which one name above all others is permanently associated, that of William Stroudley. No other railway had its locomotive works located in a popular seaside town, and it was as though Stroudley wanted to spread the sunny influence of

▲ LSWR Drummond 4-4-0 No. 310 (Class T9 rebuilt without water-tube firebox, and with superheater and stovepipe chimney).　　　　[C. C. B. Herbert

▼ LSWR Drummond large-boilered 4-4-0 No. 421 (Class L12, 1904) on up express from Ilfracombe. This engine was involved in the Salisbury derailment in 1906.　　　　[F. E. Mackay

▲ LSWR Drummond large-boilered 4-4-0 No. 467 (originally Class D15, 1912, rebuilt without water-tube firebox and with superheater as Class D15s).

[Loco. Publishing Co.

▼ LSWR: Drummond's mammoth 4-cylinder 4-6-0 No. 330 (Class F13, 1906).

[Loco. Publishing Co.

▼ LSWR: Drummond's second 4-cylinder 4-6-0 series, No. 457 (Class G14) on an up West of England express.

[F. E. Mackay

▶ LSWR: Drummond's third 4-6-0 series, No. 443 (Class T14, 1911), nicknamed the "Paddleboxes" because of the large continuous splashers, also on the West of England main line.

[F. E. Mackay

Brighton over Southern England when he decided on a brilliant gamboge yellow as the colour of his locomotives, with crimson lining, copper chimney caps, and a distinctive name for every engine, tender and tank alike, goods locomotives only excepted. Moreover, in these days long before any general "common user" of locomotives, engine-crews had their own engines, and were expected by Stroudley to keep them in first class running order and appearance, even to the extent of drivers having their names painted inside the cabs of their locomotives.

With little doubt Stroudley's most famous design was his B1 0-4-2, of which 36 were built between 1882 and 1891. The 0-4-2 wheel arrangement for tender engines was not unique, of course; Adams of the London & South Western had started building his "Jubilee" 0-4-2s for mixed traffic as far back as 1887. But what was unique was the evolution of an express passenger 0-4-2 type with front-coupled wheels of as large a diameter as 6ft 6in. With their $18\frac{1}{4}$in × 26in cylinders and 150lb pressure, the B1s shouldered much of the Brighton express work for a number of years, and a few lasted on into Southern Railway days; No. 618 *Gladstone* is still preserved in its original livery in York Railway Museum. At the other end of the Stroudley scale were the diminutive A1 and A1X 0-6-0 tanks, only 28 tons in weight, and affectionately known as the "Terriers". Built between 1872 and 1880, many of them were eventually dispersed to various lines needing light-weight locomotive power, and some are still in existence.

Stroudley reigned at Brighton from 1870 to 1889, and in 1890 was succeeded by R. J. Billinton. It was two years before the first Billinton design

appeared from Brighton Works, his Class D3 0-4-4 tank, but the main interest was now to centre in his first express passenger design, the B2 4-4-0, which in 1893 for the first time introduced the leading bogie to the LBSCR, and transferred the coupled wheels to the rear end of the engine. It also brought in what for some time to come was to be the characteristic Brighton 4-4-0 outline, with the running-plate rising in a double curve from immediately behind the buffer-beam, and being carried high above the bogie wheels and well over the coupled wheels back to the cab.

So began a lengthy series of 4-4-0s, gradually increasing in size to the B4s, of which No. 70 *Holyrood* was responsible on July 26, 1903, for working the Pullman Limited (three cars and two brakes) from Victoria to Brighton in 48min 41sec, touching 90 mph at Hawyards Heath. Only a few months earlier the same engine had worked the 08.45 from Brighton to London Bridge in 56min with a load only just short of 400 tons, developing a maximum effort of over 1,200 ihp.

In the following year, 1904, Billinton was succeeded by Douglas Earle Marsh, who had served under H. A. Ivatt of the Great Northern Railway at Doncaster, and arrived at Brighton with the drawings of the GNR Class 251 Ivatt Atlantics in his pocket. Losing no time in adapting the cylinder dimensions from $18\frac{3}{4}$in × 24in to $18\frac{1}{2}$in (later 19in) × 26 in, and the working pressure from 175 to 200lb (to permit more rapid acceleration from stops and slacks), Marsh had his first Brighton Atlantics, Nos. 37 to 41, on the road by the end of 1905. By July, 1911, a second series, Nos. 421 to 426, was beginning to emerge from Brighton Works, now with 21in cylinders and superheaters, and a more shapely outline, particularly an

▲ SR rebuild of a T14 6ft 7in 4-6-0, No. 459, with firebox water-tubes removed and superheater added, on a down Bournemouth relief express. [C. R. L. Coles

▼ One of the numerous LSWR Drummond 0-4-4 tanks, No. 42 (Class M7, 1899), passing Waterloo with a suburban train.   [Loco. Publishing Co.

improvement on Billinton's hideous chimney. Marsh had ceased the naming of Brighton engines, and the Atlantics did not receive titles until Southern Railway days, when they were named after headlands round the south coast. Another change affected by Marsh, which was regretted by many, was his abandonment of Stroudley's gamboge yellow livery for a more sober umber brown.

The next of Marsh's locomotive developments was destined to bring his name into considerable prominence. He had designed a 4-4-2 tank of which 20 in all were built, of Classes I1 and I2, in 1907 and 1908, for heavy suburban service. But they proved hopeless steamers, and were heartily disliked by their crews. But not so with the I3s, which followed in 1908, with coupled wheels increased in diameter from 5ft 6in to 6ft 9in (later 6ft 7½in), but above all with Schmidt superheaters, which transformed their performance out of all knowledge. The "Sunny South Express" had started running between Liverpool and Manchester and Brighton, with engines normally changed at Willesden Junction, but for a trial period in 1909 it was arranged that the London & North Western "Precursor" 4-4-0 *Titan* should work the train through from Rugby to Brighton, what time Earle Marsh's 4-4-2 tank No. 23 was conducting the opposite working through from Brighton to Rugby. The train was of moderate weight only, 250 tons, but was booked non-stop over the 77.2 miles between Willesden and Rugby at 52.6 mph down and 53.9 mph up.

▲ The "Bug", Drummond's LSWR 4-2-4 combined tank engine and inspection cab.   [P. Ransome-Wallis

▼ LSWR Urie 4-6-0 No. 748 *Vivien* (Class N15, precursor of the King Arthur class) on a West of England express.   [F. E. Mackay

▲ LSWR Urie mixed traffic 4-6-0 No. 489 (Class H15, 1914) on a down stopping train near Hook.

[M. W. Earley

▼ LBSCR Stroudley Terrier tank No. 40 *Brighton* (Class A1, 1878), awarded a Gold Medal at the Paris Exhibition of that year.

[Loco. Publishing Co.

▲ LBSCR Marsh 4-4-2 No. 37 (Class H1, 1906) on a Victoria–Brighton express passing Balham.

[F. E. Mackay

With her bunker heaped up to about $3\frac{1}{4}$ tons, No. 23 had no difficulty in making the *return* Brighton–Rugby–Brighton journey without re-coaling, at a cost of about 27lb of coal per mile, and without any facilities for picking up water she could run the 90 miles from East Croydon to Rugby on her tank capacity of just over 2,000gal. Superheating could not possibly have had a finer advertisement; from the thermal efficiency point of view the LNWR "Precursor" was completely outclassed, and the immediate result was the production at Crewe of the superheated "George the Fifth" 4-4-0s; and many other superheater experiments elsewhere. For some years from 1908 on, the I3 and I4 Marsh 4-4-2 tanks worked many of the expresses between Victoria and Brighton, and also had no difficulty in operating such a schedule as that of the 13.35 from Victoria to Portsmouth, non-stop over the 84 miles from Clapham Junction to Fratton in 110min, a light train certainly but over the heavily-graded mid-Sussex line.

Marsh's final production, in 1910, was the largest and heaviest locomotive which up till then had run on Brighton metals. It was originally intended to be No. 36, an "I4" 4-4-2 tank, but turned out to be No. 325 *Abergavenny*, an 89-ton 4-6-2 tank with 21in × 26in cylinders, 6ft $7\frac{1}{2}$in coupled wheels and 170lb pressure, followed two years later by No. 326 *Bessborough*, of the same type. Chief

Mechanical Engineers of the Brighton line were not a long-lived race, however, and Earle Marsh lasted only from 1904 to 1911, when he suddenly disappeared from the scene, ostensibly on the ground of ill-health.

From the beginning of 1912 his place was taken by Lawson Billinton, son of R. J. Billinton and steeped in Brighton traditions. Under him, up to the end of LBSCR history in 1922, the railway's locomotive stock reached its highest state of efficiency. His *chef d'oeuvre* with little doubt was his magnificent series of 4-6-4 express tank engines, Nos. 327 to 333, built in stages from 1914 to 1922, with 22in × 28in cylinders, 6ft 9in coupled wheels, 170lb pressure and a weight of 98 tons— some of the most handsome locomotives that have ever run in Great Britain. Some trouble was caused at first by swaying of the engines when the big side tanks were half full, but this was cured by cutting down the water space, though without any alteration to the attractive external appearance of the engines. It was little short of a tragedy when twenty years later they were converted to 4-6-0 tender engines, whose performances were far inferior to those of the engines in their original state.

Another major Lawson Billinton success was his K class, of which the first, No. 337, appeared in 1913, but the last, No. 353, not until 1922 because of delay due to the 1914–1918 war. These intro-duced the 2-6-0 wheel arrangement to the Brighton line, and with their 21in × 26in cylinders and 5ft 6in coupled wheels were equally at home on fast

freight duty, excursion trains and a variety of other tasks. Finally, mention must be made of Lawson Billinton's rebuilding with superheaters of the B4 4-4-0s, which as Class B4X were among the most capable 4-4-0 engines in the country at that time.

We come now to the South Eastern & Chatham Railway locomotive stock, which up to 1899 comprised the engines of two different companies —the London Chatham & Dover and the South Eastern. Until the end of SECR history, in part because of the weakness of underline bridges, nothing larger than 4-4-0 passenger and 0-6-0 freight tender engines, and 0-4-4 and 0-6-0 tanks, appeared on its metals. London Chatham & Dover engines, mostly from outside builders but some constructed at the company's own Long-hedge Works (almost next door to the LSWR Nine Elms Works in south-east London), were super-vised from 1874 to the end of independent LCDR history by William Kirtley, and were of simple and straightforward design, well maintained and doing admirable work over a very heavily graded main line. An almost equally long reign was that of James Stirling on the South Eastern Railway at Ashford Works, from 1878 to 1898. The dis-tinguishing feature of his engines was their stark

▲ From the second batch of Marsh LBSCR Atlantics, No. 424 (Class H2, 1911), renumbered 32424 in the BR list, on a special Pullman express. [O. J. Morris

and uncompromising outline, with the domeless boilers affected by all three Stirling brothers, carrying the safety-valves above the middle ring of the barrel, and with nothing graceful about their framing, splasher and cab design.

A radical change was destined to take place after the fusion of the two companies into the South Eastern & Chatham Railway, when in 1899 Harry S. Wainwright was appointed Locomotive, Carriage & Wagon Superintendent of the new company. In appearance his first express engines, the Class D 4-4-0s, of which in all 51 were built between 1901 and 1907, were about the most utter contrast to the Stirling domeless 4-4-0s as could possibly be imagined. The graceful lines of the former, especially of their flowing brass-beaded splashers, were enhanced by copper chimney caps, brass domes and safety-valve casings, and a marvellous livery of light green, edged by broader bands of a lighter green with yellow and red lining. However costly this finish may have been, like Stroudley's gamboge yellow on the Brighton it played no small part in brightening up rail transport in Southern England.

▲ LBSCR Marsh 4-4-2 tank No. 22 (Class 13, 1908) of the highly successful series that helped to popularise superheating in Great Britain, here heading the "Southern Belle". [H. M. Madgwick

▼ LBSCR Marsh 4-6-2 tank No. 326 *Bessborough* (Class J, 1912) heads the down "Southern Belle" past Balham.

◀ LBSCR, L. B. Billinton's handsome 4-6-4 tank No. 327 (Class L, 1914), one of the largest and heaviest tanks ever built for British use, passes Balham on a Victoria–Brighton train.   [Loco. Publishing Co.

Immediately after Wainwright's arrival, ten 4-4-0 engines that had been built in Scotland by Neilson Reid for the Great North of Scotland Railway, and to that company's designs, proved superfluous to requirements and came on the market. They were snapped up by the SECR, which was temporarily short of power, and so took up service in south-east England, complete with all their characteristic GNSR features, including cabs with two side-windows. They worked mainly over the Chatham line, and latterly from the Medway shed at Gillingham. Then the Ds were succeeded from 1905 to 1909 by the E class 4-4-0s, slightly modified by an increase in cylinder diameter from 19in to $19\frac{1}{4}$in, a decrease in coupled wheel diameter from 6ft 8in to 6ft 6in, and the first installation on the SECR of Belpaire fireboxes, with the grate area increased from 20 to 21.15sq ft. Pressure went up from 175lb to 180lb. Some of the graceful adornments of the D class had vanished, particularly when from 1908 extended smoke-boxes began to be fitted. Nos. 36 and 175 of Class E were the first SECR locomotives to receive superheaters, in 1912, when their cylinder diameters were increased to $20\frac{1}{2}$in but their working pressure was lowered to 160lb, and eventually the whole class followed suit.

In 1913 Wainwright decided on an entirely new departure for the South Eastern & Chatham, and, indeed, for all three railways that were to come into the Southern group, and that was a powerful 0-6-4 tank for outer suburban work. Only five of these J class engines were built, and they superseded a previous plan for an 0-6-2 tank type. The 0-6-4s had $19\frac{1}{2}$in × 26in cylinders, 5ft 6in coupled wheels, Belpaire fireboxes and superheaters; they weighed $70\frac{3}{4}$ tons apiece. This was Wainwright's last design, as he retired in 1913; a much larger 4-4-0 express passenger design, Class L, by then was on the drawing board, but it was left to his successor, R. E. L. Maunsell, to supervise its construction in 1913. As Maunsell's reign at Ashford was destined to continue after the formation of the Southern Railway in 1923, the very considerable developments during his *régime* are dealt with in the next chapter.

◀ LBSCR L. B. Billinton's mixed traffic 2-6-0 No. 339 (Class K, 1914); the second dome housed the top feed equipment.   [E. R. Wethersett

7 · *The Maunsell Era*

JUST AS the tenure of office by Locomotive Superintendents of the London Brighton & South Coast Railway proved to be relatively short, that of South Eastern & Chatham locomotive chiefs and their predecessors was of considerable length. As we have seen, William Kirtley presided over London Chatham & Dover locomotive fortunes for 24 years, James Stirling over those of the South Eastern Railway for 20 years, Harry Wainwright controlled South Eastern & Chatham locomotive affairs for the first 14 years of that company, while Richard Edward Lloyd Maunsell was destined to be Chief Mechanical Engineer to the SE&CR for the remaining 9 years of its life, and from then on to control the entire Southern Railway stock until 1937, a total period of 24 years in office. It was at Ashford Works that he established his headquarters.

Maunsell was fortunate in taking up his duties just at the time when the SECR Civil Engineering Department had completed the first stage of a long-needed bridge-strengthening on its main lines. As yet this was not sufficient to permit the use of 4-6-0 locomotives, but it did allow for increased weights, and it was in anticipation of this greater freedom that Wainwright had put in hand the design of the L class 4-4-0s. Under Maunsell 12 of these were supplied by Beyer Peacock in 1914, and in the same year, as no other British maker could promise early delivery, a contract for ten went to the German firm of Borsig, of Berlin-Tegel, and was finished just before the outbreak of the 1914–1918 war. As compared with the 52¼-ton E class 4-4-0s the L weighed 57½ tons, and the adhesion weight went up to 37¾ tons; cylinders were 20½in × 26in and coupled wheels 6ft 8in in diameter; with superheating the working pressure was kept down to 160lb.

The war now held up some further developments, but not completely so, for by 1917 Maunsell had produced two entirely new designs, both heavier and more powerful than anything that had appeared previously on South Eastern & Chatham metals. The first was a 2-6-0 of Class N, a design which proved so successful that eventually no fewer than 80 of these engines were built. With 19in × 28in cylinders, 5ft 6in coupled wheels, 25sq ft of grate and 200lb pressure, together, needless to say, with superheating, these proved very capable machines. The first of them weighed 61¼ tons but the later examples 64¼ tons. In 1922 Maunsell produced a variation by fitting No. 822 with three 16in × 28in cylinders, but only five were turned out at that time with this equipment.

The other new 1917 design was a massive 2-6-4 tank for main line passenger service, No. 790; no more of this Class K appeared until 1925, but in that year and 1926 a further 20 were turned out of Ashford Works. The boiler, motion and cylinders were standard with those of the N class Moguls; and one, No. 890, was fitted with three cylinders, similarly to 2-6-0 No. 822. In working order the weight of each 2-6-4 tank was 82½ tons. A break with SECR tradition was in naming these tanks after various rivers on the system.

In 1927 the "River" class earned some unenviable notoriety because of the derailment at speed of No. 800 near Sevenoaks when hauling a

▼ LCDR Kirtley 4-4-0 No. 162 (Class M, 1877) with its neat outline. [Loco. Publishing Co.

▲ SER The gaunt outline of a Stirling Class F 4-4-0, here seen at the head of some spartan SER rolling stock.
[Loco. Publishing Co.

▼ By comparison, the graceful lines of Wainwright's first SECR 4-4-0s, No. 145 (Class D, 1903).
[Loco. Publishing Co.

down Folkestone and Dover express. Suspicion was cast by some on the fact that the engine had a leading pony truck rather than a bogie, but this was proved to be unfounded when Sir Nigel Gresley of the London & North Eastern Railway, many of whose designs incorporated pony trucks, offered to try one of the "River" tanks on the reverse curves of the East Coast main line at Offord, then under a 70 mph restriction. The tank, with Gresley on the footplate, was tested at up to 83 mph with no untoward results.

There is little doubt that the real reason for the Sevenoaks derailment was poor track maintenance, and this was confirmed by the fact that the Southern Railway forthwith put in hand very heavy reconstruction and new drainage of its main lines. There had been other derailments of the "Rivers", however (though in almost every case attributable to track), and to allay public disquiet the decision was reached to convert all the 21 2-6-4 tanks to 2-6-0 tender engines, transferring them to Class U (except the 3-cylinder No. 890, which joined Class U1).

Maunsell was the first British Chief Mechanical Engineer outside the Great Western Railway to

▼ An intruder from Scotland. SECR No. 677 (Class G, 1899), a Great North of Scotland type taken over by the SECR at a time of locomotive shortage.
[Loco. Publishing Co.

take note of and to apply the Churchward principle of long-lap long-travel valves, making it possible to work locomotives economically with wide open regulators and short cut-offs. The "River" tanks and U class Moguls were so designed, and Maunsell then set about improving the performance of other Southern Railway classes by similar treatment. Among these were the Urie N15 4-6-0s of the former London & South Western Railway, which he transformed with long-travel valves, his own in place of Eastleigh superheaters, and in appearance by the substitution of handsome flared chimneys for the original stovepipes. The working pressure went up from 180 to 200lb/sq in. The Knights of the Round Table provided names for the famous "King Arthur" class, as they became, and their work from then on was of the highest quality.

The first were new engines, Nos. 448 to 457; then the Urie N15s, Nos. 736 to 755 were taken in hand and modified; while in 1925 and 1956 a new series from 763 to 806 was built for service on the Eastern and Central Divisions, the former at long last having had its Folkestone and Dover main line bridgework strengthened sufficiently to bear 4-6-0 locomotives. The Chatham section still required restricted weights, and in 1926 a superheated version of the L class 4-4-0s, Class L1, 15 in number, was built, with $19\frac{1}{2}$in × 26in cylinders,

▲ SR Maunsell development of the Class L 4-4-0s, No. 755 of Class L1, 1926, which shouldered much of the Eastern Section main line work until the underline bridges had been strenghtened   [W. J. Reynolds

6ft 8in coupled wheels, 22.5sq ft firegrate area and 180lb pressure; each of these engines weighed $67\frac{3}{4}$ tons. Further to improve the East Kent locomotive stock, Maunsell also rebuilt the Wainwright D and E class 4-4-0s, with superheaters and improved valve-setting, turning them into extremely competent machines for their size and weight.

The demand for power was steadily increasing, and resulted in the appearance in 1926 of four-cylinder 4-6-0 No. 850 *Lord Nelson*. An unusual departure from conventional practice was that the cranks were so spaced as to give eight separate impulses for each revolution of the coupled wheels, with a view to providing the maximum possible evenness of the torque; but this was done at the cost of fitting a separate Walschaerts motion for each cylinder. In view of the severe weight restrictions still laid down by the Chief Civil Engineer, the utmost care was taken in the design to keep weight to a minimum, by the use of alloy steels and in other ways, with the astonishing result that the four-cylinder *Lord Nelson* in working order was only $3\frac{1}{2}$ tons heavier than a two-cylinder "King Arthur" 4-6-0, $83\frac{1}{2}$ tons as compared with an average of 80 tons. With four $16\frac{1}{2}$in × 26in cylinders, 6ft 7in coupled wheels, and 220lb pressure, *Lord Nelson* had a nominal tractive effort of 33,510lb, and this fact was destined to have a surprising result.

Two years previously the claim of the Great Western Railway at the Wembley Exhibition that their 4-6-0 *Caerphilly Castle* was the most powerful express locomotive in the country, thereby exceeding the power of the London & North Eastern Gresley Pacific *Flying Scotsman* on the neighbouring stand, had led to the historic GWR–LNER locomotive exchange of 1925. On the basis of the tractive force formula the GWR were entitled, with their 225lb pressure, to make the claim for their "Castle", whose 31,625lb tractive effort compared with the 29,835lb only of the Pacific, with its 180lb pressure. Moreover, the results of the exchange vindicated the claim. But now, in 1926, the Southern Railway had produced a 4-6-0 with a tractive effort of 33,510lb. Despite the fact

▲ SR Maunsell's first 2-6-0 type, No. 810 (Class N, 1917). [Loco. Publishing Co.

that the effectiveness of the tractive effort figure is entirely dependent on the steam-producing capacity of the boiler, the effect of the *Lord Nelson* figure on Great Western prestige was such as to prompt pressure from the highest GWR quarters on Swindon Works to produce something still more powerful, and the upshot, of course, was the advent from Swindon in 1927 of the 4-6-0 *King George V*, with 250lb pressure and a tractive effort of 40,000lb!

The "Lord Nelson" design was involved in another controversy. The GWR–LNER loco-motive exchange of 1925 had been followed by another between the Great Western and the London Midland & Scottish Railways in 1926, in which the overwhelming superiority of the "Castle" per-formance to that of the LMSR "Claughton" 4-6-0s made it imperative for the latter company to do something drastic, and urgently, to keep pace with increasing traffic demands. Efforts were made by the LMSR to obtain from Swindon working drawings of the "Castle" design, but were met with a polite refusal. Maunsell of the Southern Railway was more accommodating, however, and the "Lord Nelson" drawings were loaned, and

undoubtedly played a part in the hurried design of the LMSR "Royal Scot" 4-6-0s of 1927. But this loan also led to some acrimonious exchanges between E. S. Cox of the LMSR and H. Holcroft of the SR as to the extent that the SR design had been *copied* by the former company, and especially that of the firebox.

One often wonders if the "Lord Nelson" 4-6-0s ever fully satisfied the aims of their designer. Seldom has a class of no more than 15 engines been subjected to so many experimental modifica-tions. No. 859 was tried with 6ft 3in as compared with 6ft 7in coupled wheels, to encourage more rapid acceleration. No. 865 had its cranks re-set from the original 135deg spacing to the more normal 180deg of four-cylinder engines, with four instead of eight exhausts to each driving wheel revolution. No. 857 received a larger diameter boiler, with round-topped instead of Belpaire firebox, pitched up to the extreme limit of the loading gauge, and later No. 860 was reboiled similarly. Maunsell studied the possibility of turning one of the engines into a four-cylinder

35017
35
BOURNEMOUTH
BELLE
35017

S4274
24
PULLMAN
PULL

▲ The experimental big boiler Lord Nelson 4-6-0,
No. 857 *Lord Howe*, of Maunsell's Class LN (1926).

[P Ransome-Wallis

▲ Britain's most powerful 4-4-0s, the Southern Schools, of Maunsell's design. This is No. 922 *Marlborough* (SR Class V, 1930). [British Railways

compound, following the success of compounding in France, but although the design reached an advanced stage, it was not proceeded with. By and large, however, the "Lord Nelson" class cannot be regarded as one of Maunsell's major successes.

Not so, however, with his next design, the "Schools" class, which were among the most competent 4-4-0 express engines ever to run on British metals. The Traffic Department was requiring some locomotives capable of working trains of up to 400 tons at 55 mph average speeds and No. 900, Class V, first of a series of 40 engines introduced from 1930 onwards, was Maunsell's reply. Again civil engineering considerations had a cramping effect, especially the restricted clearance tunnels on the Hastings line, which made necessary the use of round-topped fireboxes and a rounded cab profile, but every difficulty was overcome brilliantly.

To reduce hammer-blow and permit an adhesion weight up to 42 tons, three-cylinder propulsion was adopted; three $16\frac{1}{2}$in × 26in cylinders, 6ft 7in coupled wheels and 220lb pressure gave a tractive effort of 25,130lb, and a firegrate of no less than 28.3sq ft helped to ensure an ample supply of steam. These 67-ton 4-4-0s could equal the performance of any "King Arthur" 4-6-0, and some of their feats are almost legendary, such as that of No. 931 in working a 305-ton train from Waterloo to passing Grateley, 72.8 miles, in 64min, or of No. 932 in running a 15-coach train of 473 tons tare

▲ For short distance express passenger work—No. 890 *River Frome*, one of the SR Maunsell 3-cylinder 2-6-4 tanks of Class W, later converted to tender 2-6-0s.
[Loco. Publishing Co.

and 510 tons gross (three coaches over the maximum rostered load for this timing) from Waterloo to Southampton in 86min 32sec, 1min inside schedule.

A useful new Maunsell design which appeared in 1929 was his Class Z 0-8-0 shunting tank, with three 16in × 28in cylinders to provide a high tractive effort. An unusual feature of these engines was the concentration of their $71\frac{1}{2}$ tons weight on a wheelbase of only 17ft 6in, which entailed a considerable overhang at both leading and trailing ends. Among other construction at this period was a further series of three-cylinder Class U (16in × 28in) 6ft Moguls, with 220lb pressure, whose high tractive effort made them suitable for a considerable variety of duties; on test the three-cylinder engines showed a coal consumption 12 per cent less than the two-cylinder variety.

In his final years of office Maunsell had some notable plans in hand, but always it was the limitations imposed by the Chief Civil Engineer that prevented them from coming to fruition. One was for a four-cylinder Pacific, uniform with a "Lord Nelson" 4-6-0 as far back as the coupled wheels, but with a wide firebox providing a grate area of 40sq ft. It would have been an enormously long machine, with an engine wheelbase of 37ft 6in, and an overall length, with six-wheel tender, of 72ft 7in over buffers. A shorter alternative would have been a three-cylinder 2-6-2, also with wide firebox, but neither was destined to materialise. When, under Maunsell's successor, a Pacific eventually did appear on Southern metals, it was in every possible respect a totally different machine. So, in 1937, there ended the career of a Chief Mechanical Engineer which, if it did not perhaps reach the highest pinnacle of success, nevertheless had a profoundly beneficial effect on the locomotive stock of the Southern Railway.

8 · *The Bulleid Revolution*

IF EVER the epithet "sensational" could be applied to the work of a Chief Mechanical Engineer, a strong contender for the distinction undoubtedly could have been the late O. V. S. Bulleid of the Southern Railway. Perhaps "controversial" would be a kinder description; during his twelve-year reign at Brighton Works, which later he made his working headquarters rather than Ashford or Eastleigh, he produced no more than four new designs, but each one of them in a number of details was a radical departure from all previous precedents. During his 25 years' service at Doncaster, the last fourteen as Personal Assistant to Sir Nigel Gresley, Bulleid could and did act in an advisory capacity, but with no power of independent action, and always under the shadow of a very distinguished Chief; but once installed in the seat of Southern locomotive authority, at the personal invitation of Sir Herbert Walker, he had a freedom of action that was untrammelled by any restrictions other than those still imposed by the Chief Civil Engineer.

The effects of this freedom on a very adventurous mind were destined to be startling indeed. "Unbridled licence" is the description given by E. S. Cox in his book *Speaking of Steam* to Bulleid's reign; the latter was the last of all British Chief Mechanical Engineers to enjoy such liberty, and he certainly made the most of it, in some directions to the advantage of steam locomotive design, but in others with principles not fully thought out and inadequately tried out, which ultimately proved very costly to the Southern Railway.

The first new engines to be built under Bulleid actually were of a design prepared by R. E. L. Maunsell just before his retirement; these were a series of 0-6-0s, Class Q, 20 in number, with 19in × 26in cylinders, 5ft 1in coupled wheels, 200lb pressure, and a weight of $49\frac{1}{2}$ tons in working order. With their tractive effort of 26,150lb, these were easily the most powerful Southern 0-6-0s to take the rails up to that date; moreover they had a handsome and impressive appearance, in complete contrast to their immediate Bulleid-designed successors, the Q1s.

One experiment of this period is worth mention. On the London & North Eastern Railway Bulleid had had a good deal to do with the streamlining of Gresley's A4 Pacifics for the "Silver Jubilee" and other streamline trains. So in 1939 he had "Schools" class 4-4-0 No. 935 dressed up in a flashy mock-up streamlining, of a character typical of the period. But nothing permanent came of it.

Bulleid's first production design of his own aroused a vast amount of controversy. It was his "Merchant Navy" Pacific, which appeared from Eastleigh Works in 1941, in the middle of the 1939–1945 war. Briefly, the features which differed totally from accepted British locomotive

▼ The ultimate in ugliness—Bulleid's Class Q1 0-6-0 (1942), most powerful 0-6-0 type in Britain, pared of all superfluous details to save weight. No. C23 on a freight in the Bournemouth area.　[H. Weston

practice were the all-welded steel firebox fitted with thermic syphons; the valve-motion enclosed in an oil-bath and operated by a chain; solid steel wheel centres of the Boxpok type; and no reciprocating balance, the three-cylinder propulsion being relied on for an even torque. Over the boiler and motion was wrapped a thin steel casing, the locomotive being described as "air-smoothed" rather than streamlined. A new system of numbering was adopted, the first of these 4-6-2s being No. 21C1, the "C" for three coupled axles, the "2" for the bogie, and the "1" for the trailing pair of wheels; one might have considered that "2C1-1" would have been more logical, but the designer thought otherwise.

Now what about the effect of these departures from traditional practice? The Bulleid all-welded boiler proved an unqualified success; comparative tests at the Rugby testing-plant showed it to have a steam-raising capacity superior to that of any other contemporary type. At first corrosion of the steel fireboxes proved a menace but then Bulleid decided to experiment with the French TIA (*Traitement Intégrale Armand*) feed-water treatment, first tried at Ramsgate depot, where the water was very hard, and this proved so successful in reducing boiler maintenance costs that in a modified form it became standard Southern practice.

But the chain-driven valve-motion, enclosed in an oil-bath, was another matter. With the "Merchant Navy" Pacifics, each chain had 118 links, and though the chains themselves did not stretch, the cumulative wear of pins and holes resulted in an eventual lengthening of the chains by as much as 6in. As a result, any kind of precision in operation was impossible. In the tests of No. 35022 on the Rugby plant, one day on 10 per

▲ As originally built—No. 21C3 *Royal Mail*, of the first series of "Merchant Navy" Pacifics (Class MN, 1941).
[British Railways

▼ A "Merchant Navy" Pacific as completely rebuilt under British Railways auspices—No. 35018 *British India Line*.
[British Railways

▲ The impressiveness (though not the economy!) of steam traction. "West Country" Pacific No. 21C139 climbing out of Victoria with an express to the Kent Coast. [Eric Treacy

cent cut-off the engine showed a bigger drawbar pull at 15 to 20 mph than it had done previously on 15 per cent, while on the following day the pull at 15 per cent was doubled. I believe it has not been unknown for a "Merchant Navy" Pacific to move forwards when nominally in backward gear and *vice versa*! The oil-bath also gave a great deal of trouble; it could not be kept oil-tight, and not only did this mean an excessive consumption of lubricant, but spraying of oil over the track gave the engines an unenviable reputation for slipping, and also several times caused the boiler lagging of a Pacific to catch fire. Again, the inaccessibility of the motion increased the time required at the sheds for maintenance.

So it was that the Bulleid Pacifics, though on their emergence much admired by the management, proved a good deal less than popular at the locomotive depots, even though some of the difficulties were overcome with experience. But with the engine-crews it was another matter. Never before had they had in their charge machines which even on so difficult a route as that from Salisbury to Exeter could be relied on to keep time in any condition of loading; and the 4–6–2s were always extremely speedy engines, notwithstanding coupled wheels no more than 6ft 2in in diameter. Maximum Southern speeds in those days were limited to 85 mph, but in the last few months before electric working began between Waterloo, Southampton and Bournemouth the Pacific drivers took liberties, and speeds up to and exceeding 100 mph, even on level track, were by no means uncommon.

Also the crews appreciated the regard for their comfort that Bulleid had had in designing their cabs; one novel feature was the pedal on which the fireman could tread, as he swung his shovel round from the tender to the firehole, to open the firedoor automatically for him.

Drivers did not appreciate, however, the tendency of the exhaust to drift down from the chimney and obscure the cab front windows; an almost endless series of modifications of the front end casing were tried, but there was no complete cure until after Bulleid's departure the air-smoothed casings were removed in the complete rebuilding of the engines by British Railways.

In the locomotive exchange of 1948, following on nationalisation, the Bulleid Pacifics greatly distinguished themselves, beating many of their rivals in the matter of times and speeds; but this was largely because their crews were determined to keep time or improve on it at all costs, whereas the drivers of certain other types made coal economy their main aim, with poor performances as a result. But the Bulleid engines paid for their exploits by some of the highest coal consumptions of the whole series. They showed some of the best boiler efficiency figures, but what they gained here they lost by lower efficiency at the front end.

The first five "Merchant Navy" Pacifics came out in 1941; ten had been completed by August 1942, but it was not until April 1949 that the last of the 30 engines was at work. There was not a little

▲ A roving commission—"West Country" Pacific No. 34006 *Bude* beating all competitors in time between Marylebone and Manchester in the 1948 Locomotive Exchange, seen here near Northwood with dynamometer car.   [C. R. L. Coles

public criticism that high speed passenger engines of such a kind as this should take precedence in construction at this critical time in the 1939–1945 war, and also of the elaborate naming ceremonies which followed the emergence of each new engine. In view of the maritime associations of the Southern Railway the names were those of shipping lines associated mainly with Southampton.

In the middle 1940s the SR Traffic Department was needing some lighter main line locomotives, which could be used when necessary over weight-restricted routes, and also on a variety of branch services. Something a little more powerful than the Moguls would probably have met the case, but Bulleid thought otherwise. Instead, there appeared in November 1945 the first of no fewer than 110 light Pacifics, of which some certainly took a share in the harder main line duties, but many were destined to spend much of their time working two-coach or three-coach trains over branches in the West Country. How Bulleid managed to justify so costly a proceeding at such a time with the Southern Railway Board, and, no doubt, with the Ministry of Transport, will always remain a mystery.

For the "West Country" and "Battle of Britain" Pacifics incorporated just the same expensive features of design as their bigger brothers. As compared with the three 18in × 24in cylinders of the "Merchant Navy" Pacifics, those of the light 4-6-2s were 16⅜in × 24in; the 6ft 2in coupled wheel diameter of both types was the same, as also the working pressure of 280lb/sq in. It was rare,

however, for drivers to use steam-chest pressures anything like as high as 280lb; much of the work of the 4-6-2s was done with partially closed regulators and pressures in their steam-chests of not much more than 150lb or so. To conform to the limits laid down by the Chief Civil Engineer, all kinds of expedients were used to keep down the engine weights; each "Merchant Navy" Pacific in working order turned the scale at 94¾ tons, but a "West Country" Pacific weighed 86 tons only.

After Bulleid had left British Railways in 1948 for Ireland, trouble developed in 1953 with the crank axles of the "Merchant Navy" Pacifics, necessitating withdrawal for repairs on such a scale that at one time no fewer than 37 locomotives had to be borrowed from other BR Regions to keep the main line services going; they included such distinguished strangers as standard "Britannia" Pacifics and Eastern Region 2-6-2s. Shortly afterwards a vital decision was reached by the locomotive authorities of British Railways.. It was that, in view of the high cost of coal, lubricating oil and maintenance incurred by the Bulleid 4-6-2s they should be completely rebuilt.

The re-design was skilfully carried out by R. G. Jarvis, Chief Technical Assistant at Brighton Works, and the first rebuilt "Merchant Navy" 4-6-2 began service in February 1956. The air-

▲ Bulleid's revolutionary 0-6-6-0 "Leader" tank—
No. 36001 under the tests which did not succeed in
saving the design.   [British Railways

smoothed casing has been removed, a new smoke-box had been provided, Walschaerts valve-motion had been substituted for the chain-driven variety, and the working pressure had been reduced to 250lb. Tests showed that these and many other changes had substantially improved the thermal efficiency of the class, and had changed its performance from the previous uncertainty to complete predictability, but it had been a very costly conversion to have to make. All the "Merchant Navy" 4-6-2s were rebuilt, and 60 out of the 110 light Pacifics. It is only fair to add that not a few of the engine-crews regretted the change, and considered that they could get better work out of the engines in their original form.

Between the two Pacific series another remarkable Bulleid design had appeared, and that was his Q1 0-6-0, to which reference has been made already. The 1939–1945 war was well under way when the first of these incredibly ugly machines made its appearance in 1942. As an austerity measure Bulleid decided to dispense with any running-plate round the engine; the flat-sided casings of smokebox, barrel and firebox were perched high above the coupled wheels; the squat, large-diameter stove-pipe chimney crowned a multiple-jet exhaust; and the appearance in general was bizarre in the extreme. So much so, indeed, that when Sir William Stanier of the LMSR first saw a photograph of one his terse comment was: "I don't believe it!" These 40 engines, with their 19in × 26in cylinders, 5ft 1in coupled wheels, and 230lb pressure were probably the most power 0-6-0s in the country, yet weighed no more than 51¼ tons apiece.

Mention of the multiple-jet exhaust is a reminder that this was a Bulleid speciality, as compared with the double blast-pipes and double chimneys that were becoming popular on other lines. All the Bulleid Pacifics were equipped with the former, and Bulleid then treated many of his predecessors' locomotives similarly, to the great advantage of their steaming. With other modifications, more particularly of the valve-setting, the Maunsell "Lord Nelsons" reached the highest performance level of their history after this treatment. All the "Schools" 4-4-0s also were equipped with multiple-jet exhaust, but in this case the improvement in performance was obtained only at the cost of a sad disfigurement, with their enormous new chimneys, of what had been a very handsome design.

We come lastly to Bulleid's most extraordinary design exploit, and that was his "Leader" tank. Here again the Traffic Department was in need of some modern tank locomotives rather more powerful than existing 0-6-0 tanks, for freight transfer duties; and this revolutionary machine was Bulleid's reply. The use of sleeve valves in a steam locomotive was not new; it had been tried in the Midland Railway 2-6-2 No. 2299, built at Derby in 1909 to the design and largely at the expense of Cecil Paget, the General Superintendent (and over the head of R. M. Deeley, the Chief

Mechanical Engineer). After completion, this 2-6-2 made some trial runs, but serious troubles with the valves caused the project to be abandoned. Bulleid, however, having made some preliminary experiments with SR Atlantic No. 2039 *Hartland Point*, decided to proceed with his plan. As compared with Maunsell, who usually experimented for a year or two with a new locomotive type before setting out to multiply it, Bulleid had no such inhibitions, and before any experience whatever had been gained with a design which in every possible respect was to be totally new, decided to lay down at Brighton frames for no fewer than six of these unique "Leader" tanks.

Limitations of space make it impossible to describe in detail all the unique features of the "Leader" tank; those who would like fuller information not only about this locomotive but about Bulleid's work in general should consult the book, *Bulleid, Last Great Giant of Steam*, written by Sean Day-Lewis. In brief, the tank had the 0-6-6-0 wheel arrangement, with chains replacing normal coupling-rods; the whole locomotive body was perched high above a massive girder frame measuring 67ft over buffers, with the entire 120 tons weight available for adhesion. Each bogie was fitted with a three-cylinder double-acting simple expansion engine, driving a three-throw middle crank axle. There was continuous pump-driven flood lubrication for each engine and all moving parts. The all-welded boiler was offset on the

▼ Improvements in efficiency by Bulleid with standard classes. No. 850 *Lord Nelson* fitted with Lemaître exhaust and large-diameter chimney, on a down Continental express near Hildenborough.
[Loco. Publishing Co.

main frames, to permit of a side corridor connecting the front and rear driving cabs, but this made the locomotive undesirably lopsided in weight. Weighting the corridor side to compensate increased the total weight, which already was 10 tons over the estimated figure. The fireman occupied a separate compartment in the centre, from which he could see nothing outside, and in which it was proved by experience that the temperature could rise as high as 120°F—a pretty insupportable condition for any length of time.

When the first "Leader" emerged from Brighton Works, on June 21, 1949, the Southern Railway had lost its identity in the national system; and three months later Bulleid had retired. Two of the "Leaders" were actually completed; and the building of no fewer than 35 was threatened; but it would have meant months and months of patient and costly experiment before any practical results could have been anticipated. Tests were continued for a time, but as it was calculated that already some £150,000 had been spent without any fruitful result on the project, the new locomotive authorities of British Railways regretfully decided that the experiment must be abandoned, and the two completed "Leaders" were therefore broken up. Again to quote E. S. Cox, Bulleid "aimed at the stars, and controversy has raged, and still rages, as to how far he hit the target and how far he fell short". Nevertheless, it would be idle to deny that in the technical realm more progress has been made by breaking away from tradition than by sticking rigidly to it; given a little more careful thought and a little more time, Bulleid might have made an unassailable name for himself as a great locomotive engineer.

9 · Southern Passenger Rolling Stock

It MUST be confessed that in general none of the constituent companies of what was to become the Southern Railway, in their earlier years at least, had much to boast about in their passenger rolling stock. Some of it, indeed, was spartan to a degree, like that of the London Chatham & Dover Railway, which almost to the end of that company's independent existence consisted mainly of four-wheelers. With the London Brighton & South Coast Railway bogie stock was fairly late in making its appearance, and corridor trains on both the South Eastern & Chatham and Brighton lines were practically unknown until the time of the grouping.

One reason, of course, was that neither of these companies ever built any restaurant cars, so that corridors were unnecessary for access purposes, and would have been uneconomical as cutting down seating accommodation. The London & South Western Railway, however, with its longer journeys to and from Bournemouth and the West of England, had introduced its first restaurant cars by 1901, as part of new five-coach trains for the West of England service, in which the kitchens shared one of the end vehicles with van space.

Long before this, however, a beginning had been made in the matter of first class comfort by the introduction of Pullman cars. Actually in Great Britain it was the Midland Railway which took the lead in this matter, bringing into service the first Pullman cars—"drawing room" cars by day, converted to sleeping cars by night—between St. Pancras and Bradford in 1874. In 1875 one of these cars, the *Mars*, gravitated to the London Brighton & South Coast Railway, and worked as a parlour car between London and Brighton until in 1877 it removed to Italy and there became a sleeping car once more. But then the LBSCR started Pullman operation in earnest, and gradually became a user on an extensive scale.

In 1875 even the London Chatham & Dover Railway acquired the Pullman car *Jupiter*, but was so unaccustomed to such luxury that nine years later the car was transferred to the LBSCR. In 1889, in connection with the Great International Exhibition in Paris, the LCDR had another try, with a "Club Train" composed of cars built on the Continent to the order of the International Sleeping Car Company, which connected at Dover with a special cross-Channel steamer; and to preserve its reputation the South Eastern followed suit. The service did not pay, and was withdrawn in 1893.

Two years earlier, however, the SER had made a surprise move. It was to acquire from the Gilbert Car Manufacturing Company of the USA some really luxurious first class drawing room cars, which at first worked singly, but in 1896 were added to and formed into a six-car luxury train carrying not only first, but also second and third class passengers between Charing Cross and Hastings, and, moreover, without any supplementary fares. Such was the success of the experiment that in 1897 a similar train, this time built in England by the Metropolitan Carriage & Wagon Company, was installed between Charing Cross and Folkestone, with the imposing title "Folkestone Vestibuled Limited". Oddly, no Folkestone or Dover boat train had any special provision for the comfort of Continental travellers (apart from the unsuccessful "Club Trains") until the first Pullmans were introduced on this route in 1910.

In 1880 the London & South Western Railway experimented with a Pullman car between Waterloo and Exeter, but for a couple of years only; not until 1890 was there a more permanent Pullman introduction, on several trains between Waterloo and Bournemouth. In the first decade of the century both Pullman and restaurant cars were running in certain Bournemouth trains, but about the years 1911 and 1912 the LSWR Pullmans were made over to the LBSCR, and Pullmans were not seen again on South Western metals until the installation of the all-Pullman "Bournemouth Belle" in 1931.

The first all-Pullman train in the country seems to have been a set of four cars that started to run between Victoria and Brighton in December, 1881. It was notable in that the parlour car *Beatrice* was equipped with what was probably the first electric lighting of a railway coach in history, with current supplied from a battery of 32 accumulators; to charge these a special steam-driven dynamo was installed at Victoria. This train was followed in 1888 by a new set of cars, which were lighted throughout by electricity; in this case the versatile William Stroudley, the LBSCR Locomotive, Carriage & Wagon Superintendent, had devised what was probably the first installation on record of an axle-driven dynamo to supply the current, located in a six-wheel van specially shaped and painted to be uniform with the Pullman stock. Two of these vans were built, and by the irreverent were christened "Pullman Pups". In addition, the

cars were equipped with the new Pullman vestibules, so that this was among the first trains in the country, if not the first, to provide enclosed communication of a corridor train between its coaches.

By 1898 the "Sunday Pullman Limited" had begun to run regularly between Victoria and Brighton, and soon attracted so much patronage as to require six or seven cars; in the following year it was renamed the "Brighton Pullman Limited". Ten years later it became a daily all-Pullman service, operated twice in each direction daily with a handsome train of new 12-wheel cars, and a new name. the "Southern Belle", still first class only. Eastbourne also acquired an all-Pullman Sunday service, the only train ever scheduled to run regularly between Victoria and Eastbourne without any intermediate stop. In course of time, to make better use of the train paths involved, the "Southern Belle" ran with ordinary coaches of both classes attached, but the Brighton electrification of 1933 saw the introduction of the two-class "Brighton Belle", for which three five-car Pullman sets were turned out; they included the only motor-driven pre-war Pullmans ever built. Soon the "Belle" required ten cars daily, and eventually it was making four return journeys each day, until by reason of age there came the much-lamented disappearance of the train in 1972.

Other all-Pullman trains by degrees were introduced to the Southern services. The year 1929 saw the introduction of the "Golden Arrow" between Victoria and Dover, first class only; by 1951 a handsome new train of Pullmans of both classes had taken the rails. This had been preceded in 1931 by the "Bournemouth Belle", at first running on Sundays only non-stop between Waterloo and Bournemouth West, but from 1936 a daily service, calling also at Southampton. For many years this was a very popular train, normally composed of ten cars, but at times growing to eleven or twelve.

It disappeared on the introduction of electric working in 1967. In 1931, also, Pullmans began to run in the boat trains between Waterloo and Southampton.

Next, in 1947, came the "Devon Belle", running at summer week-ends only between Waterloo and both Ilfracombe and Plymouth. Its normal formation was twelve cars, occasionally increased at peak periods to as many as fourteen, and including in each train a Pullman that had been rebuilt as an observation car, the only such cars ever to run on the SR. But patronage of the train proved disappointing as the post-war motoring habit bit into BR's domestic holiday market, and it was withdrawn in 1954. Then as far back as 1921 the South Eastern & Chatham Railway had tried the experiment of a Sunday Pullman Limited between Victoria, Margate and Ramsgate; this lasted for a short time only, but in 1948 the Southern Railway inaugurated a new "Thanet Belle" Pullman, which by 1949 was operating daily, with a through Canterbury portion and renamed the "Kentish Belle". The 1959 electrification saw the end of this service also.

During all these years Pullmans had been introduced on such a scale in Southern England that the great majority of the trains between Victoria (and some to and from London Bridge) and Brighton, Eastbourne, Worthing and Bognor included at least one Pullman; others were run in the Newhaven boat trains; also in the expresses between Charing Cross and Folkestone, Dover, Deal and Hastings; and between Victoria and the Kent Coast. The total number of Southern Pullmans in use ultimately must have been considerable; but in later years the introduction of pantry-equipped first class coaches foreshadowed the miniature buffets and

▲ A Hastings express of the SECR, showing the "birdcage" which was a typical feature of SECR guards' vans. The engine is No. 763 of Class L.

[F. E. Mackay

▼ A Victoria–Brighton express of the former LBSCR, composed of "Balloon" stock (so named for the highly arched coach roofs). The locomotive is No. 60 of the rebuilt and capable B4x class.

[O. J. Morris

buffet cars that by 1972 had completely displaced the whole of the Pullman fleet.

The amount of space devoted in this chapter to Pullman operation is due to the fact that apart from these luxury cars the various constituent companies had built little rolling stock that was worthy of remark. No corridor coaches, other than those of its Royal train, were ever built by the London Brighton & South Coast Railway; its only coaches of unusual design were the so-called "Balloon" non-corridor sets of 1905, with their high arched roofs, for the Victoria-Newhaven boat service, and a few for push-and-pull trains, which were not perpetuated because their height restricted their use.

It was not until two years before the end of its independent existence that the South Eastern & Chatham built its first corridor trains for the Victoria-Dover boat service, in one respect odd because the brake coaches had no vestibules at their outer ends. In some earlier SECR non-corridor stock what would otherwise have been

▲ Maximum accommodation in minimum length—
Bulleid's experimental double-deck suburban train.
[British Railways

two or three compartments in the centre of certain coaches were opened out to form a first class saloon; a similar saloon was provided in the end brake coaches of the new boat trains. In 1930 some new "nondescript" coaches of first class standard were built for the boat trains which could be changed at will into first, second or third class according to traffic flows, but eventually became standardised as second class. One feature of South Eastern & Chatham rolling stock that continued to the end of that company's history was the provision of raised "bird-cages" above brake-van roofs to enable guards to see out over the roofs of their trains.

On the London & South Western Railway, as noted already, the first corridor trains had come into use by 1901, and as their use extended, it was indicated in the timetables by the words "Luncheon Corridor Express" or variations to suit the meal that was being served. By 1903 some unusually luxurious stock, by LSWR standards, had been built for service between Plymouth and Waterloo, for the boat trains that were to be run in connection with the forthcoming calls of Transatlantic steamers at Plymouth; and these included the only sleeping cars ever to run on Southern metals. But well into Southern Railway history many main line trains, particularly to and from Bournemouth, were still formed of non-corridor stock.

With R. E. L. Maunsell in office as the first Chief Mechanical Engineer of the Southern Railway, however, the building of corridor trains began on a much more extensive scale. Coaches of three different widths were turned out—9ft for general use, 8ft 6in for the Thanet lines, with their more restricted clearances, and straight-sided 8ft 6in vehicles for the Charing Cross–Hastings line, with its one or two very narrow tunnels. It is always a mystery why the Southern Railway and later British Railways have never faced the widening or opening out of these tunnels, which not only have necessitated the use of this narrow rolling stock, but also have prevented electrification and made it necessary to build special diesel-electric trains for this route only.

If nothing startling had happened to coach design up to the end of R. E. L. Maunsell's period of office as SR Chief Mechanical Engineer, it was a different matter altogether when he had been succeeded in 1937 by O. V. S. Bulleid, who was as adventurous with some of his passenger stock as he was with his locomotive designs. The most remarkable experiments that he made were with his restaurant cars. First, in 1938, came some buffet cars for the Bognor service, with pedestal seats facing outwards along a long counter, a blank wall behind, and an interior of distinctly Moorish aspect. Later versions had normal windows, each with a curved table encircled by four ordinary chairs.

But the greatest novelty appeared in 1949. New restaurant cars were required for the "Atlantic Coast Express", and it was arranged that these should be built at Eastleigh not only for the train concerned, but for certain well-known Eastern Region trains also. So we witnessed the emergence of Bulleid's famous "Tavern" car sets. The

"Taverns" were kitchen cars of which one end was arranged to provide the atmosphere of an English "pub"—mock Tudor beams, oak panelling, leaded lights, settles, refectory-like tables, the lot. Coupled to each tavern car was the restaurant car, with tables and seats facing inwards along the two walls, and small windows so high up that no one could see through them. The height of fatuity was reached by painting an inn sign outside each tavern, and colouring the exterior steel panelling of each coach to resemble red brickwork, with plaster and beams above. In next to no time these sets, the restaurant cars in particular, had become so unpopular that rebuilding on more conventional lines became imperative.

All this time, however, Bulleid was turning out corridor rolling stock with a high standard of appearance and comfort, and there was also, in his last year of office, a suburban development of note. This was a four-coach set of double-deckers, in an attempt to meet the tremendous commuter demand on the Eastern Section lines without further lengthening of the trains. The coach interiors were most ingeniously designed, with upper and lower seating sections dovetailed into one another in such a way as still to keep the coach roofs within the narrow limits of the SR loading gauge. But the experiment failed because it was impossible for these coaches to fill and empty within the normal brief station stops.

All through the periods described in this chapter, the building of coaches for suburban service from 1909 onwards by the constituent companies, and of corridor stock for successive main line electrifications by the Southern Railway from 1932 onwards, had proceeded on a vast scale; indeed, it is probable that from 1909 to the end of Southern history this coach output must have been greater than that of any other of the British railway groups.

▼ The observation car of the all-Pullman "Devon Belle".   [British Railways

▼ Sightseeing in comfort—interior of the "Devon Belle" observation car.   [British Railways

10 · *The Development of Passenger Services*

SOME EARLY speed possibilities exhibited by constituent companies of the Southern Railway were connected with the opening of a new hotel at Ramsgate called the Granville, and the competition between the South Eastern and London Chatham & Dover Railways to provide access to it. In 1877 the hotel proprietor persuaded the SER to run a special train on Friday afternoons, non-stop over the 85 miles from Cannon Street to Ramsgate via Tonbridge and Ashford; though advertised to take 2¼hr, such a brilliant trial run was made in 1¾hr that by April 1878 the time had been cut to 1hr 55min. On Monday mornings the return journey was scheduled to take 2hr 10min. The down journey schedule required an average of 48.6 mph, which was brilliant for the period. The train was called the "Granville Express", and it was probably the first train in Great Britain to carry an official title. But intermediate stops were soon inserted, and ten years later the overall average speed had dropped to 40 mph.

Not to be outdone, the London Chatham & Dover Railway in April 1878 inaugurated a "Granville & Westgate-on-Sea Special Express" train, conveying all three classes of passenger and running daily. Leaving Victoria at 15.15, after calling at Herne Hill for its Holborn Viaduct connection, it had a non-stop booking at 46 mph to Westgate, and with stops at Margate and Broadstairs was due in Ramsgate at 17.15. The return working left Ramsgate at 10.00 on a similar 2hr journey to Victoria. This train was a much more permanent institution, and soon also assumed the title "Granville Express" after the SER train had lost its name and its supremacy. It is remarkable that after all but a century, and now with electrification, the best time between Victoria and Ramsgate is still no better than 1hr 53min by the hourly trains, and 1hr 48min by the best evening train (or 1¾hr from Cannon Street), compared with the LCDR 2hr, though the trains of to-day, of course, have many more intermediate stops.

On the London Brighton & South Coast Railway in these earlier years there was nothing that could be called fast. In general, the 51-mile journey between London and Brighton took 70 to 80min, but for this apparent sloth there was some excuse, as until the opening in 1900 of the Quarry line between Stoats Nest and Earlswood, avoiding Redhill, all LBSCR trains had to use the original line through Merstham, heavily congested because of all the South Eastern Railway traffic. Even before this, however, in 1898, the "Sunday Pullman Limited" had introduced the first 60min timing between Victoria and Brighton, though many more years were to pass before 60min runs became general.

One notable train of these early years was the "City Limited", which, having originated in 1841 with a 1¾hr timing, by 1862 had come down to 70min from Brighton to London Bridge, but had to wait until 1912 before being accelerated to 62min up and 60min down. At the beginning of the century this was one of the heaviest regular formations in the country, notwithstanding the fact that it carried first class passengers only. In the up direction, leaving Brighton at 08.45, the main London Bridge portion comprised six bogie firsts and three 8-wheel Pullmans, with 6-wheel brakes at each end, while the Victoria portion had two bogie firsts, a 12-wheel Pullman and another 6-wheel brake. On Mondays an additional bogie first was run in each section, and the entire train then totalled 17 vehicles, 67 axles, weighing 348 tons empty and at least 370 tons full—a tremendous task for the locomotives of the period, which were never double-headed. The down "City Limited", at 17.00 from London Bridge, without a Victoria portion, was of course lighter.

On the up journey the Victoria coaches were slipped at East Croydon, while from 1865 onwards the 17.00 was slipping coaches, first at Three Bridges and later at Haywards Heath. This is a reminder that the LBSCR was the first railway, not only in Great Britain but in the whole world, to detach coaches at intermediate stations from trains passing at speed. The practice appears to have begun in 1858 with coaches for Lewes detached at Haywards Heath from the 16.00 from London Bridge to Brighton. At the end of the same year the Great Western Railway started slipping coaches at Slough and Banbury, and so began a practice which up to the outbreak of the 1914–1918 war attained very considerable dimensions in Great Britain, but now has ceased entirely because of the cost of providing specially-fitted stock and an additional guard for each slip portion.

Any deficiences in the speed of its neighbours' trains were not shared by the London & South Western Railway. As early as 1899 the LSWR had introduced the first non-stop runs between Waterloo and Bournemouth, at 16.10 from

Waterloo in 2hr 6min—a notable feat in that in the absence of track water-troughs the locomotives had to make the run of 107.9 miles on a single supply from the tender water-tanks, which was why the LSWR quite early introduced high capacity bogie tenders. This acceleration took place during the brief reign as Superintendent of the Line of the forceful Sam Fay, who in later years was to earn considerable notoriety as General Manager of the Great Central Railway. By 1911 the non-stop Waterloo–Bournemouth time in each direction had come down to the even 2hr. Competition with the Great Western Railway also produced fast timings over the West of England main line, with such timings as 91min for the 83.8 miles from Waterloo to Salisbury, and 96min over the heavily-graded 88.0 miles from Salisbury to Exeter.

What the LSWR could do in the realm of speed was amply demonstrated in the LSWR-GWR competition from 1903 onwards for the traffic from Plymouth to London off the Transatlantic steamers which had begun making calls in Plymouth Sound, the LSWR bringing up the passengers and the GWR the mails. The zenith of LSWR achievement was reached on April 23, 1904, when the

▲ An unusual locomotive-changing point—Bulleid Pacific No. 35003 *Royal Mail* starting the "Devon Belle" from Wilton after taking over from No. 35008 *Orient Line*.　　　　　　　　　　　　　[L. Elsey

▼ In full flight near Winchfield—the "Atlantic Coast Express", headed by "Merchant Navy" Pacific No. 21C9 *Shaw Savill*.　　　　　　[M. W. Earley

LSWR special ran from Stonehouse Pool at Plymouth up to Waterloo, 231 miles, in 4hr 2¾min, with a signal stop at Exeter St. Davids and a change of engines at Templecombe. The 112.2 miles from Templecombe to Waterloo were covered in 104min 33sec. No stop was made at Salisbury, and this fact led eventually to the disaster of 1906, when (as was not unusual) the boat train ran through Salisbury station at much too high a speed but was derailed on the sharp curve immediately beyond, with considerable loss of life.

A feature of the South of England train services in the first decade of the century was the development of through train services between the North and Midlands and the South Coast resorts. This was long before the day of the family motorcar, and families appreciated the convenience of being able to travel from north to south and *vice versa* without having to cross London. This facility was most used during the summer season, of course, but throughout the year such facilities became popular with many travellers. The earliest, promoted by the Great Central Railway in order to bring patronage to its newly-opened London Extension, and worked by trains of its own stock, was in 1902 between Newcastle-on-Tyne and Bournemouth, via York, Sheffield, Banbury, Oxford and Basingstoke, in which North Eastern, Great Central, Great Western and London &

South Western motive power were all involved. Next, inaugurated in 1903, was a through service between Birkenhead, Dover and Deal, worked by the Great Western Railway through Birmingham and Oxford to Reading, where the South Eastern & Chatham took over for the continuation through Guildford and Redhill to Folkestone, Dover and Deal.

Then, in 1904, there came the "Sunny South Express", initially of through coaches only but from 1905 onwards a fully-fledged restaurant car express, operated by the London & North Western Railway with its own stock between Liverpool, Manchester and Willesden Junction, where the London, Brighton & South Coast took over to work the train through to Brighton and Eastbourne. The idea proved infectious, and soon through coaches were being run to and from the Kent Coast from both the Midland and Great Northern Railways, by way of the Metropolitan Snow Hill connection to Herne Hill; one daily service in 1914 brought together at Herne Hill coaches from all three Northern railways into a single multi-coloured assemblage which was run by the SECR through to Ramsgate.

Between the wars, at weekends, these through workings expanded into a whole series of trains between the North and the Midlands and the various south-east and south coast resorts; but then by degrees, with the spread of motorcar travel, most of the through trains were reduced to weekend workings only. By 1973 sole survivors were one daily through train between Newcastle, Bournemouth and Poole, now from Sheffield to Banbury by way of Derby, Birmingham and

▼ Maximum task for a Southern "Schools" 4-4-0— No. 927 *Clifton* passing Clapham Junction on the 108-mile non-stop run of the "Bournemouth Limited" from Waterloo to Bournemouth.

[British Railways

▲ At Worting Junction—Rebuilt "Merchant Navy" Pacific No. 35010 *Blue Star* switches the "Bournemouth Belle" over to the Southampton line.
[British Railways

Leamington, as the Great Central route no longer exists; and another between Liverpool, Crewe, Birmingham, Oxford and Poole. Two other trains operated between Birmingham, Poole and Southampton, and there were a number of Saturday workings in summer to and from Poole and Weymouth, but none to and from the Central and Eastern Divisions.

Early in 1921 the London & South Western Railway took a very important step; it was to establish Britain's first even-interval main line train service. From now on expresses left Waterloo throughout the day at 30min past each hour for Bournemouth, those at 30min past the even hours

calling at Southampton and taking $2\frac{1}{4}$hr; for the West of England they started at the even hours; and for Portsmouth at 50 min past each hour. Later in the same year the Great Western Railway began a similar and even more comprehensive timetable arrangement, which applied to up as well as down trains, but to the LSWR belongs the credit for having been the first to introduce an even-interval timetable arrangement, which is now the standard practice over almost every main line in Great Britain, and on a scale far more extensive than in any other country in the world.

While steam still reigned over the Southern main lines, acceleration took place by degrees, but not on any spectacular scale. Between the wars the first 80min timings were introduced between Charing Cross and Folkestone Central, and were restored after the 1939–1945 war; for a short time

▲ Stroudley 0-4-2 *Jonas Levy* passes Balham in LBSCR days with the "Sunny South Express", composed of London & North Western stock. [Loco. Publishing Co.

▼ The "Sunny South Express" leaving Eastbourne, in charge of Billinton 4-4-0 No. 323 *William Cubitt* (Class B2) of the LBSCR. [Loco. Publishing Co.

before electrification the 16.15 from Charing Cross and the 11.10 from Folkestone received the name "Man of Kent". By now this had become a corridor train with two Pullman cars, and was a happy hunting-ground for the 4-4-0 "Schools". Similarly what had been the "Granville Express" right up to the outbreak of war in 1939 was maintaining its 90min schedule from Victoria to Margate, and with a corridor formation of up to nine to eleven coaches, including Pullmans, was no light problem of haulage over this 73.9 miles of severe gradients. But no timing as fast as 90min has reappeared since the war, not even with electrification.

On the Western Section the non-stop Waterloo–Bournemouth expresses in Southern days had acquired the title "Bournemouth Limited", and their timings had been pared to 116min down and

118min up. As mentioned earlier, it was on this working that the "Schools" displayed their maximum powers, and performed work which for 4-4-0 locomotives was brilliant in the extreme. Records show that *King's Wimbledon* once worked a 10-coach train of 345 gross tons up over the 107.9 miles in 108min net, and *Malvern* a heavier 12-coach load of 415 gross tons in $114\frac{1}{2}$min net— and this with a water supply limited to the 4,000gal capacity of the tender tank. The "Bournemouth Limited" was withdrawn on the outbreak of war in 1939, and after the war Southampton had become a stop of such importance that there have not since the war been any more non-stop Bournemouth runs. In 1951, in honour of the Festival of Britain, another express on this service received a name—the "Royal Wessex", up from Bournemouth at 08.40 and down at 16.35—but this was

▲ Maunsell's 2-6-4 tank No. 801 *River Darenth* heads the through GWR-SECR Birkenhead–Dover express, mainly of GWR stock.   [M. W. Earley

▼ A Victoria–Brighton express of the LBSCR passing Wandsworth Common behind Billinton Class B4 No. 52 *Siemens* (of the same type as No. 70 *Holyrood*, which made the record London–Brighton run in 1903).   [F. E. Mackay

after nationalisation and the schedule was not notable for speed.

On the West of England main line the 11.00 from Waterloo in 1927 received the name "Atlantic Coast Express", and so became the Southern "ACE". Like its chief competitor, the Great Western "Cornish Riviera Express", the "ACE" was one of the two most multi-portioned trains in the country, with through coaches for Seaton, Sidmouth, Exmouth, Exeter (the restaurant cars), Ilfracombe, Torrington, Bude, Padstow and Plymouth. Salisbury was the first stop, and here engines were changed until the advent of the Bulleid "Merchant Navy" Pacifics, with which through working to Exeter began.

But the "Atlantic Coast Express" had to wait until after nationalisation, in 1952, before a notable speed-up took place, with no more than 83min allowed for the 83.8 miles from Waterloo to Salisbury, and 80min for the 75.9 miles of stiff gradients on to Sidmouth Junction, cut nine years later to 80min and 75min respectively. These were the first mile-a-minute bookings to appear in the Southern timetables, and 75min down and 74min up over the 75.9 miles between Salisbury and Sidmouth Junction were the fastest bookings ever entrusted to British steam power over gradients of such severity. But the Bulleid Pacifics had no difficulty in keeping and even improving on these schedules.

One more working over this main line that was of interest was the "Devon Belle Pullman". Introduced in the final year of Southern Railway history, it was shown in the timetable as non-stop from Waterloo to Sidmouth Junction, but actually required an intermediate stop for change of engine. This was not made at Salisbury, but at one station further on, Wilton. The "Devon-Belle" was not noted for speed, but it certainly was for weight. At the short lived peak of its popularity it occasionally reached a total of fourteen Pullmans, with a tare weight of 545 tons and a gross weight of at least 575 tons—a vast tonnage to be handled over the 1 in 80 gradients west of Salisbury. But again the Bulleid Pacifics covered this assignment without any great difficulty.

On the Central Section there were no timetable changes of note until 1933 saw the inauguration of electric working between London, Brighton and Worthing, with Eastbourne and Hastings following in 1935, and the Western Division Waterloo–Portsmouth line in 1937. In these and the later electrifications even-interval times became standard, with considerable additions to and acceleration of the trains, such as the provision of hourly 60min expresses between Victoria and Brighton. But the other main line electrifications in Southern England came after the end of Southern Railway history.

To describe in detail the effect of electrification on the London suburban services of the Southern Railway and its predecessors would be impossible within the limits of space available. Rapid acceleration with electricity made substantial acceleration possible over all the lines concerned; the trains became far more frequent; and even-interval train times throughout the off-peak hours became a *sine qua non*. In the peak hours the commuter demand has now developed to the stage that scarcely another train can be packed on to the densely-crowded lines, and very substantial expenditure has become an absolute necessity to provide the urgently needed relief.

▼ The ten-car "Southern Belle" Pullman, at speed behind Lawson Billinton 4-6-4 tank No. 328 (later rebuilt as a 4-6-0 tender engine). [Loco. Publishing Co.

11 · *Electrification*

As HAS been mentioned earlier, the Southern Railway by the conclusion of its history could claim the most extensive electric suburban railway system owned by any individual railway in the world. From its predecessors the SR on its formation in 1923 took over 74 electrified route miles of line, comprising 242 miles in all of electrically-equipped track; by the end of its reign, in 1947, the total had grown to 706 route miles and 1,760 track miles. Since nationalisation these totals have been greatly added to by the main line extensions to Margate, Ramsgate, Folkestone and Dover, and to Southampton and Bournemouth, but these are beyond the scope of the present volume.

The first Southern Railway constituent to feel the threat of electricity was the London, Brighton & South Coast. Early in the century there had been a proposal for a high speed electric railway from London to Brighton. This prompted the very fast runs made experimentally by 4-4-0 No. 70

Holyrood on July 26, 1903, when three Pullmans and a van were hurried from Victoria to Brighton in 48min 41sec, with top speeds of 80½ mph at Horley and 90 at Haywards Heath, and minima of 58 mph at Quarry Tunnel, 66½ at Balcombe Tunnel and 69 at the exit from Clayton Tunnel. The return journey was made in 50min 21sec, with a maximum speed of 85 mph. The Bill submitted to Parliament promised London–Brighton 50min journeys, but was defeated, and with little doubt this demonstration of the possibilities with steam traction had some influence on the result. So steam was destined to continue in possession of this main line for another thirty years.

A worse preoccupation of the Brighton authorities at this time, however, was the competition now being offered to its suburban traffic by the London County Council, South Metropolitan and Croydon Corporation electric trams, which by 1903 were proving highly popular with the public. Obviously the only effective reply by the LBSCR must be electric traction. In this decision the Brighton proved a good deal more farseeing than either of its neighbours—the South Eastern & Chatham and

▼ The original London Brighton & South Coast overhead ac electrification—a suburban train at Victoria.　　　　　[Loco. Publishing Co.

▼ One of the motorcoaches of a push-and-pull LBSCR train set with overhead ac conduction. [H. C. Casserley

▲ Class "E2" No. 104, on a down Crystal Palace train, near Honor Oak Park. [O. J. Morris

▲ The most multi-tracked stretch of running lines in Great Britain—18 tracks (including one or two sidings) at the approach to Clapham Junction; left and centre, LSWR, and right, LBSCR. [British Railways

London & South Western Railways. It called in Philip Dawson (later Sir Philip), an eminent electrical and traction specialist, to report on how to tackle the problem. Although the first electrified sections of London's Underground as well as certain lines round Liverpool already were operating with third-rail or fourth-rail dc conduction, Dawson's report of 1904 recommended the Brighton management to opt for single-phase overhead conduction, using 6,700 volts ac. He had in mind not only the London suburban area, but also the main line to Brighton and the coast line from there to Worthing and Portsmouth.

Dawson's recommendation was accepted, and the first section to be electrified was the 8¾-mile South London line between London Bridge and Victoria. The first equipment was ordered from the German AEG firm in Berlin, and the work was completed in 1909. So serious had been the tram competition that whereas in 1902, the last year of horse trams in South London, the bookings at Peckham Rye (to take a typical South London station) had totalled 1,213,281, by 1908, the last year of steam traction, they had dropped to 526,373. But in their first year the electric trains restored the figure to 1,051,263. For all the stations between London Bridge and Victoria there was a fall from roughly 8,000,000 passenger bookings to 3,000,000 between 1903 and 1908, but there was a recovery to 8,000,000 by 1910, while immediately before the grouping the total had risen to 12,000,000.

Thus encouraged, the Brighton next electrified the lines from Battersea Park to Crystal Palace Low Level and on to Norwood Junction, with the Peckham Rye–Dulwich–West Norwood line, brought into use in 1912, though it was not until 1925, after the 1914–1918 war, and now under Southern Railway auspices, that further extensions of the overhead electrification were completed from Balham through East Croydon to Coulsdon North, and from Norwood Junction through West Croydon to Sutton.

Meantime, however, the Brighton's neighbours at last had bestirred themselves to realise their equal need of electrification. One wonders what might have happened had they followed the Brighton example of overhead ac conduction, but the urge to conform to what was becoming a general fashion was too strong, and it was third-rail dc electrification that was decided on. It should be interpolated here that actually the first London & South Western electric constituent had been the Waterloo & City Railway, with third-rail dc conduction; with experience already available from tube lines already in operation this had been built and equipped as a tube line on its opening in 1898. So far as concerns surface lines, however, it was not until shortly before the outbreak of war in 1914 that the South Western started work on its suburban electrification, and the war was well under way when the first LSWR electric network was brought into service in 1916. This was from Waterloo to Wimbledon, Kingston, Twickenham and Richmond back to Waterloo, with the Twickenham–Hounslow–Brentford–Barnes loop, the Teddington–Shepperton branch, and the main line from Malden through Surbiton to terminals at Hampton Court and Claygate.

Nine years were now to elapse, during the 1914–1918 war and after, before any extensions of the electrification took place, and these were under the auspices of the Southern Railway. At last the former South Eastern & Chatham suburban lines came into the picture, electric working being brought into use between Orpington and both

▲ Bane of the Eastern Section—Borough Market Junction, London Bridge Charing Cross lines to left; Cannon Street lines to right.   [British Railways

Victoria and Holborn Viaduct in 1925, with the Hayes branch; a year later the lines between Charing Cross and Cannon Street and the same points were added, as well as to and from Dartford by the Greenwich, the Blackheath and the Sidcup lines, with various branches. At the same time electrification was extending rapidly over the former London & South Western system, 1925 seeing Raynes Park linked with Epsom, Leatherhead and Dorking, and Claygate with Guildford via Effingham Junction, with the Leatherhead–Effingham spur. Surprisingly, however, it was not until 1937 that electric operation was initiated between Waterloo and Guildford by the direct Woking route, as part of the main line electrification to Portsmouth, which was completed in that year.

Meantime a very serious question had to be settled by the Southern Railway management. Sandwiched in between their South Western and South Eastern electrifications, with third-rail dc low-voltage conduction, was the Brighton overhead high voltage ac system, and no kind of interworking between the two was possible. As we have seen, in the light of subsequent events the Brighton management had been the more farseeing of the two, but in view of the extent to which the third rail system had progressed by the middle 1920s the decision reached was unavoidable. It was that the Brighton overhead system must be converted to the third-rail system by which it was

hemmed in on both sides. The last Brighton lines to receive overhead equipment were those to Coulsdon North and Sutton in 1925; by 1929 the last overhead wires had disappeared, and third-rail dc conduction was in use on all the Southern suburban lines that had been electrified to that date.

Electrification continued to spread rapidly, and the expenditure by the Southern Railway at this time on equipment and rolling stock must have been on an enormous scale. A great day in Brighton history was January 1, 1933, when at long last, after the threat of electric competition thirty years earlier, the first electric trains from London ran into Brighton, Hove and Worthing, with Eastbourne and Hastings added two years later, and the mid-Sussex line to Horsham, Arundel, Bognor Regis, Chichester and Portsmouth by 1938. So, as mentioned already, by the close of independent Southern Railway history in 1947, its electrified system extended to a total of 706 route miles and 1,760 track miles.

In order to facilitate the working of its immense and ramified suburban service, the Southern Railway was unusually well provided with flying and burrowing junctions, as far as possible thereby to avoid trains having to cross one another's paths on the flat. Many of these avoiding lines were laid in by the predecessors of the Southern, in steam days. It was in 1862, for example, that the London Brighton & South Coast Railway started to lay out the extraordinary collection of flying and burrowing junctions at Windmill Bridge, Croydon, between the lines from London Bridge and

Victoria to the Brighton main line and to West Croydon, with double line connections in every direction and, to add to the complication, the slow lines burrowing under the fast lines in order to cross from one side of the latter to the other. Curiously enough, the only flat junction left here is one of the most important of all, and that is where the fast lines from Victoria and London Bridge join one another just short of East Croydon station.

There is another maze of lines between Vauxhall and Clapham Junction, where the former London & South Western and London Brighton & South Coast main lines come together for a short distance, and the former is crossed by the one-time London Chatham & Dover main line from Victoria and the LBSCR South London line, while the West London Extension line comes from the west to the Latchmere Junctions, and makes burrowing connections, mainly used by freight, with all of them. The West London Extension was formerly the joint property of the LSWR, LBSCR, London & North Western and Great Western Railways, and the participation of the last-mentioned was made evident by the GWR type semaphore signals which in the 1970s could still be seen from Waterloo trains where they crossed the West London Extension line just short of Clapham Junction.

Down the former London & South Western main line the first burrowing junction laid in with a branch was at Raynes Park with the up line from Epsom, in 1884; later there followed the dive-under of the down Kingston line at Malden; the flyover beyond Surbiton of the down Hampton Court line, with its imposing 155ft skew span, immediately followed by the dive-under of the up Cobham line; the dive-under at Byfleet Junction of the down line from Chertsey; the flyover at Pirbright Junction of the up Aldershot line; and specially notable, the flyover that brings the up Southampton line into the West of England main line at Worthing Junction, Basingstoke. Curiously enough, there is another important junction that has never yet been tackled in this way, presumably because it would have involved so much disturbance of existing lines and sidings, and that is the junction at Woking between the main and Portsmouth lines.

Last of all the Western Division flyovers to be built has perhaps been the most important of all. For many years the arrangement of the Western Division main line, with the fast lines in the centre and the slow lines on either side, meant that the majority of the up suburban trains (other than those from the Richmond direction) had to cross the main lines on the flat outside Waterloo. In 1936 this operating handicap was brought to an end by a new flyover at Durnsford Road, just on

▼ Slade Lane Junction, Eastern Section, with Bulleid double-deck suburban train en route for Dartford.
[J. H. Cooper-Smith

the London side of Wimbledon, which brought the up suburban line over the main lines to join the down suburban line for the remainder of the run into Waterloo, where suitable track alterations completed an improvement of great note.

The former South Eastern & Chatham line is not nearly so well provided with such junctions, and, moreover, possesses one junction which for years past has been the greatest headache on the whole system. This is Borough Market Junction, London Bridge, where trains for Cannon Street and Charing Cross part company. Congestion here was at its worst when most Charing Cross trains diverted into Cannon Street and reversed there before proceeding to London Bridge and beyond. That practice has long since ceased, and in Southern Railway days as much as possible was done, by devising parallel workings which would avoid conflicting train movements, to ease the problem. In the 1970s plans are at last finalised for complete remodelling of this junction and its approaches, but the more their implementation is protracted so much the more immensely costly the work will be.

Soon after the formation of the South Eastern & Chatham Railway in 1899 the desirability was realised of a link between the two principal main lines where they cross one another just east of Chislehurst. So, with the aid of a system of burrowing junctions to avoid any crossing of tracks on the flat, connections were first laid in from Bickley on the Chatham line to Orpington on the South Eastern, brought into use in 1902, and two years later from Chislehurst on the South Eastern to St. Mary Cray on the Chatham. The purpose was to make it possible to travel direct from any London SECR terminus to either the South Eastern or Chatham line. Since then the Bickley–Orpington spurs have been the regular route for boat trains between Victoria, Folkestone and Dover. An important improvement carried out in Southern Railway days and completed in 1933–1935 was the connection from Nunhead to Lewisham, flying over the Dover main line at Parks Bridge Junction, which made possible greatly improved electric services from Holborn Viaduct to the mid-Kent and Catford lines without any interference with the main line traffic.

With its vast suburban electric traffic, the Southern Railway had the distinction of owning the two busiest railway stations in Great Britain. It is estimated that Clapham Junction handled, and still does, over 2,000 train movements every 24hr, and London Bridge, both terminal and through, just short of that number. Waterloo, with about 1,325 trains in and out, took third place on the SR, though just beaten by the LNER terminus at Liverpool Street. The trackage at the approach to

▼ A typical Southern express from Victoria to the South Coast, made up of six-car sets, one with Pullman car and the other with pantry car, at speed on the Quarry line.   [British Railways

the Southern stations mentioned also creates a record; the combined legacy of the former South Eastern & Chatham and London Brighton & South Coast Railways still is twelve parallel tracks for a part of the first $1\frac{1}{2}$ miles out of London Bridge, while where the former London Brighton & South Coast and London & South Western lines parallel one another on the east side of Clapham Junction there are twelve running lines. It is doubtful if such a concentration can be found anywhere else in the world.

As to main lines which had been electrified by the end of Southern Railway history, these had not then extended further than from Victoria and London Bridge to Brighton, Eastbourne and Hastings, with the coast line from Ore and Hastings through Eastbourne, Lewes and Hastings to Worthing, Littlehampton, Bognor, Chichester and Portsmouth, the mid-Sussex line through Horsham and Arundel, and the direct line from Waterloo to Guildford and Portsmouth. On the South Eastern side the limits that had been reached were Sevenoaks, Chatham, Gillingham and Maidstone. The later long-distance extensions to Margate, Ramsgate, Folkestone, Dover, Deal, Southampton and Bournemouth were destined to wait until the years of nationalisation.

Finally, while O. V. S. Bulleid, the SR Chief Mechanical Engineer, was producing his highly

original steam locomotive designs, he also was showing his versatility by an uneasy collaboration with his electric rival, A. Raworth, the Electrical Engineer, in designing a main line electric locomotive for the Southern. The product emerged from Ashford Works in 1941. It was of the Co-Co type, 56ft 9in long and weighing a shade under 100 tons, and Bulleid was responsible for the chassis and body, which had several novel features. So had the electrical equipment, with a booster set between the current supply and the motors which included a heavy flywheel designed to store enough energy to keep the set running over gaps in the third rail. Current was, of course, the normal Southern 660–750V dc, with third rail conduction. Each of the six axles were separately motored; the total hp was 1,500, and the rated tractive effort 40,000lb.

No. CC-1, later 20001, was designed to handle passenger trains up to 750 tons in weight, and 1,000-ton freight trains. No. CC-2, later 20002, followed with various improvements in 1943, and a greatly modified No. CC-3 (20003) in 1948, after nationalisation. The last of the three was 58ft 3in long, and put the tractive effort up to 45,000lb. These electric locomotives found useful employment in fast freight traffic, but their principal task was the haulage of the boat trains between Victoria and Newhaven Harbour, which they performed with considerably greater load-hauling and time-regaining ability than the Brighton Atlantics that had preceded them.

▼ Diesel-electric traction. A Charing Cross–Hastings train of narrow stock (because of limited clearances) passing Orpington.   [J. H. Cooper-Smith

12 · *Southern Freight*

As MENTIONED already in Chapter 10, the Southern Railway was the only one of the four railway groups that earned a greater revenue from passenger than from freight traffic. The comparative figures are instructive. If 1932 be taken as a typical year between the wars, the London Midland & Scottish Railway earned £25,389,302 from passenger and £37,210,250 from freight traffic; with the London & North Eastern Railway the figures were £16,868,577 and £29,850,524 and with the Great Western £11,339,457 and £15,313,721 respectively. But with the Southern Railway there was a complete reversal, only £5,393,102 being earned by freight handling, whereas passenger receipts amounted to £15,597,768, well over the Great Western total and nearly equal to those of the much more extensive London & North Eastern Railway.

The reasons for this preponderance of Southern passenger revenue have been explained already. As to freight, there is no manufacturing on any large scale carried on in the Southern counties; there is a coalfield in Kent, but limited in size, and with its product, other than that required for locomotive purposes in the past by the Southern Railway and its predecessors, used in the main in Kent and the neighbouring counties, and so requiring short hauls only. The port of Southampton has generated a certain amount of traffic, but beyond that the freight carried by the Southern Railway has been mainly of agricultural products. So, as the figures in the first paragraph have shown, receipts from freight traffic in a typical year on the Southern Railways were only one-third of those on the Great Western Railway, between one-fifth and one-sixth of those on the London & North Eastern Railway, and less than one-seventh of those on the London Midland & Scottish Railway.

For this reason little that was notable in freight motive power was ever developed by the Southern Railway or its constituent companies. No eight-coupled tender freight engines were built; the only use of eight-coupled wheels in the later years was the 4-8-0 LSWR tanks Urie designed for marshalling at Feltham yard and the Maunsell Class Z three-cylinder 0-8-0 tanks for shunting work. Otherwise the SECR and LBSCR and their successors relied entirely on 0-6-0 locomotives for general freight work and 2-6-0s for mixed traffic; while the LSWR developed several series of 4-6-0 locomotives with relatively small coupled wheels for fast freight trains, in addition to the normal complement of 0-6-0s for the slower trains. As Chapter 8 has described, Bulleid's final Southern Railway 0-6-0 design, the ungainly Austerity Q1

▼ Urie's powerful 4-6-2 tank, No. 520 (LSWR Class H16) on transfer freight work between Reading and Feltham yard.   [M. W. Earley

▲ Urie's companion 4-8-0 tank, No. 492 (Class G16), engaged on working freight trains over one of the humps at Feltham marshalling yard.

[Loco. Publishing Co.

▼ Also designed for transfer work, Maunsell 3-cylinder 2-6-4 tank No. 31915 (Class W) in BR days working freight between Old Oak Common and Norwood Junction marshalling yards through Crystal Palace (LL).

[B. Stephenson

▲ **Another** Maunsell 3-cylinder tank type, primarily for shunting work—No. 30950 of Class Z, working between Southampton and Fawley.   [P. M. Alexander

▼ In double harness—two Maunsell Class W 0-8-0 tanks banking a heavy freight train up the 1 in 37 from Exeter St. Davids to Queen Street.   [M. J. Fox

type, were the most powerful locomotives of this wheel arrangement that have ever run on British metals.

The limited amount of Southern freight traffic did not call for anything exceptional in the way of marshalling yards, with one notable exception— that at Feltham. It was under the *aegis* of Sir Herbert Walker as General Manager that the London & South Western Railway decided, shortly after the end of the 1914–1918 war, to do away with a number of small yards in the London area and concentrate their work in a single mechanised hump marshalling yard. The site chosen was at Feltham, midway between Richmond and Staines on the line from Waterloo to Windsor and Reading, and no better location could have been devised. It removed all freight working from the main line between Clapham Junction and Byfleet; exchange traffic from the London & North Western, Midland, Great Northern and Great Eastern lines had easy access by way of Willesden Junction, Acton, Kew Bridge and Hounslow; exchange traffic from the Central and Eastern Divisions had equally easy access by way of the ramified Latchmere network and Clapham Junction; and the Staines–Virginia Water–Chertsey–Byfleet Junction line provided a direct route to all parts of the south and west.

The down yard at Feltham was laid out with 6 reception and 17 sorting sidings, and the up with 8 reception and 16 sorting sidings. Humps were provided for sorting, which was completely mechanised with power operation of points—one of the biggest such installations in Great Britain up to that time. And as described already, Urie designed 4-8-0 tanks for working the trains over the

humps, and 4-6-2 tanks for transfer work to and from the Midland and Northern lines. By 1922 the work of construction was completed, and from then on it was shown that up to 3,390 wagons could be dealt with in 24hr, and that a train of 70 wagons, involving 56 cuts, could be sorted in no more than 12min. Today however, the site is a trackless waste, for the yard has been eliminated in the development of British Railways' through freight train network and reduction of marshalling facilities.

The Central Division has never needed any marshalling yard on such a scale, but between Hither Green and Grove Park, on the Eastern Division, extensive marshalling operations were and still are carried out, mainly with freight traffic to and from the Midland and Great Northern lines. Formerly all these trains were worked through to and from the railways concerned by their own 0-6-0 tank locomotives, by way of the Metropolitan Snow Hill line and then the spur connecting the Holborn Viaduct and Charing Cross–London Bridge lines at Metropolitan Junction, and at one time the number of trains so operating had grown to about 40 daily.

This addition to the dense passenger services over Borough Market Junction and through London Bridge became too troublesome to continue, even though the freight workings were confined as far as possible to the slack daylight hours and the nights. Relief was finally given in 1929 by constructing new connections at Lewisham, one from the Greenwich Park line to the St. Johns–Blackheath line and the other from Lewisham Junction direct to Hither Green. This made it possible to divert the Midland and Great Northern workings through Loughborough Junction and Nunhead, greatly easing the situation.

▼ Fitted freight—Maunsell U class 2-6-0 No. 1796 at speed with a fast freight from Southampton to Feltham.   [M. W. Earley

13 · *Southern Pioneers in Signalling*

IN VARIOUS very important ways the predecessors of the Southern Railway exerted a strong influence on the development of British railway signalling, in some of which they were in fact the pioneers. By the time that the trains of four different railways were being handled at the Corbett's Lane Junction of the London & Greenwich Railway, in 1842, it became imperative to have some means of identifying them, so that the junction pointsmen might set their switches correctly. So from then on the trains were made to carry distinguishing headcodes, and a tall structure which earned the nickname "Corbett's Lane Lighthouse" was erected to watch the approaching trains and signal to the pointsmen below where they were going. It was at about the same time that the first semaphore signal arms came into use at New Cross.

The "Lighthouse" might have been regarded as the first railway signalbox, but this description really applies to the structure which appeared in 1843 at the point where the junction was laid in for the branch to the new Bricklayer's Arms terminus of the South Eastern Railway. Gregory,

the Engineer of the line, when erecting tall semaphore signals to control the junction points, decided to group the point levers in one place, with his signalman on a raised platform from which he had a clear view of the approaching trains. The next development of note occurred in 1856, and it was the subject of a patent by a man named Saxby, who was a foreman in Brighton Locomotive Works and another named Farmer, then the LBSCR Assistant Traffic Manager. It was an apparatus designed to control the working of signals and points in such a way that it would be impossible to show conflicting signal indications—in brief, the first introduction of interlocking, which has been a basic safety principle of signalling ever since. So there was formed the well-known firm of Saxby & Farmer, later amalgamated with the Westinghouse Signal Company. One of the earliest productions of this firm was a couple of signalboxes with their interlocking apparatus erected across the lines outside London Bridge Station, which for a long time afterwards set a fashion for such boxes outside all the SER, LBSCR and LSWR terminals, bridging all lines and carrying above them a fearsome array of signalposts and arms, out of which drivers had the

▼ Early South Eastern Railway signalling at Charing Cross—a typical terminal signal bridge carrying both signals and signalbox.   [British Railways

Early London & South Western signals at Waterloo.
[Loco. Publishing Co.

by no means easy task—in fog, indeed, an almost impossible one—of picking out the particular signals relating to their trains.

Also the invention of another signalling pioneer, W. R. Sykes—that of the electrically controlled lock-and-block system, forerunner of the later track circuit, was installed experimentally in 1875 at three busy London Chatham & Dover junction signalboxes in the London area, one of them at Brixton. After a disastrous collision in 1878 at Sittingbourne J. S. Forbes of the LCDR decided to apply it to the whole of his system. By 1882 it was in operation from London throughout to Dover, and later the London Brighton & South Coast and London & South Western Railways came to the same decision.

It may be added that as early as 1861 a primitive electric block system had been established on the busy Brighton main line through Clayton Tunnel; signals at each end were set automatically to danger by each passing train, and then had to be released by the tunnel signalmen after an appropriate time interval, but as a result of an electrical failure on one evening in 1861 two up trains collided in the tunnel, with the loss of 22 lives.

For another development of note the London & South Western Railway was responsible. At the close of the last century attention was being directed in the United States towards power signalling as a means of expediting signalbox work. The first railway to experiment in this direction in Great Britain was the Great Eastern, which in 1899 equipped its Spitalfields Yard Box with the McKenzie & Holland & Westinghouse electro-pneumatic system. In 1901 the LSWR followed suit with its box at Grately, between Andover and Salisbury, and a year later there came a considerably bigger installation in the principal box at Salisbury.

But this was the preliminary to an even more important development. This was the bringing into operation in 1902 of the first fully automatic main line power signalling in Great Britain initially between Grately and Andover, and shortly afterwards over the $23\frac{1}{2}$ miles between Woking and Basingstoke. The firm responsible was the British Pneumatic Signal Company. Along the four-track section just mentioned, semaphore signals were carried on gantries across all four tracks, spaced about 1,500ft apart; the four signalposts each carried a home and distant signal arms for each track, which in effect provided three positions—all

▲ Three-position semaphore signals temporarily installed at Victoria, South Eastern & Chatham side.
[Loco. Publishing Co.

arms horizontal for stop, the home arm off but distant arm on for one section ahead clear; and both arms off for two sections or more ahead clear. Normally the arms were in the off position; track circuits then returned them to danger as a train passed, and then successively returned the home signal to clear as the train passed the next gantry and the distant to clear when the second gantry ahead had been passed. Along the length of the automatically signalled section passed a pipe charged with air at 15lb/sq in pressure; this was known as a low pressure electro-pneumatic system. It did excellent service until replaced many years later by electric colour-light signalling.

Another type of three-position signalling was brought into service by the SE&CR in 1919 on their side of Victoria station, American signalling practice was beginning to favour the three signalling aspects given by three-position semaphore signals —horizontal for stop, 45deg for one section ahead clear, and vertical for two or more sections clear— instead of separate stop and distant signals—and this was the system decided on for the running signals at Victoria. The contract was placed with the General Railway Signal Company, and as the 1914–1918 war had begun, and it was not possible to obtain the components in Great Britain, the locking-frame was ordered from the Railway Signal Company of Rochester, N.Y. But the ship bringing it to England was torpedoed and sunk; the war was almost ended before a replacement had arrived, and the installation, with the three-position signals, was complete.

Apart from some of the London Underground lines, however, and one or two experimental installations elsewhere, the three-position semaphore signal did not find favour in Great Britain. It was a different matter altogether with three-position and four-position electric colour-light signals, but the Southern Railway had to wait a good many years before making a start with what is now standard signalling practice for busy lines.

One last fact connected with Southern signalling requires mention. At the start of this chapter there was description of "Corbett's Lane Lighthouse", erected at Britain's first railway junction to enable the pointsmen to recognise the destination of approaching trains, and so to set their points correctly. To help them various signs were devised to be carried by the locomotives so that their routes might be readily identified. In course of

WA125
35023

time most of the railways of Britain used engine headlamps unlighted by day and lighted by night to indicate the type of train—express passenger, stopping passenger, empty coaches, mineral, and so on—but not so the lines in the South of England. Their network was so complicated that eventually they developed an equally complicated system of head-discs by day and headlamps by night, to assist their signalmen.

In particular the London Brighton & South Coast Railway, not content with the normal four headlamp positions—base of chimney and three along the buffer-beam—added two more by tall lamp-irons, each carrying two discs or lamps one above the other at the buffer-beam ends. At one time four different types of daytime discs were in use—plain white circular, the same with a black cross, a circular disc enclosing two black diamonds and a square disc with two black cross-bars. Eventually, as it was not possible to show similar variations at night, the number of discs in use came down to two, the plain white and the white with cross, replaced at night with white and green headlamps respectively.

The London & South Western Railway similarly increased its headlamp positions to six by equipping its engines with lamp-irons on both sides of the smokebox; the LSWR also used several varieties of disc in earlier days, with a black cross on a white circle and a black centre to a white circle, but eventually came down to the plain circular white disc only. Much the same variety was found on the South Eastern & Chatham, which made extensive use of a square black disc with a white diamond painted on it. The coming of electrification gradually swept away all these fearsome head-disc and headlamp complexities, and substituted the far simpler route-numbering, illuminated at night.

So the predecessors of the Southern Railway were responsible for the first use of semaphore signal arms, the first signalbox, the first interlocking, and the first continuous main line automatic signalling—an impressive list indeed.

14 · *Across the Channel*

It was inevitable that railways with lines bordering the Channel coast would eventually become engaged in maritime activities, and to this rule the predecessors of the Southern Railway were no exceptions. The South Eastern Railway was the first to become so engaged. As early as 1843 the SER bought Folkestone Harbour for the modest sum of £18,000; immediately opposite, across the Channel, was Boulogne, and the SER management soon realised the possibilities of a direct route from London to Paris via Folkestone–Boulogne. So much so, indeed, that the English company helped to finance the Boulogne–Amiens Railway, which was soon to form a part of the main line of the Northern Railway of France.

The year in which Folkestone Harbour was purchased was the same as that in which the SER first reached that town, and to connect with the harbour a branch steeply descending at 1 in 30 was laid down to the harbour, over which by 1849

passenger trains were authorised to travel. It was little realised at the time what a handicap this gradient would prove to operation in later years, with up to four locomotives sometimes needed to push heavy Continental trains up to Folkestone Junction; at one time an easier route was planned, starting to descend west of Folkestone Central, but owing to local opposition the project was abandoned.

Development of the harbour was begun immediately, and by the early 1860s, when a new pier had been constructed at which vessels could berth at all states of the tide, some handsome new ships were making the Folkestone–Boulogne crossing at a speed of $12\frac{1}{2}$ knots. By 1876 further improvements had been effected, whereby the boat trains were now able to run alongside the ships, though as yet it could not be said that the transfer of passengers was the acme of comfort, particularly in bad weather.

All this time the South Eastern Railway, secure, as it thought, in possessing the most direct route from London to Paris, had been singularly indifferent to what was going on 7 miles away at

▼ A unique cross-Channel steamer between Dover and Calais in early days—the twin-hulled *Calais-Douvres*, of French design, built in 1878.

Dover. The Corporation of Dover was jealous of the increasing prosperity of its neighbour, but could do little about its own rather poor harbour, which was under the control of the Harbour Commissioners. However, in view of the strategic importance of Dover, in 1847 the Admiralty stepped in, and began to build a massive breakwater which it was intended should be used by the mail services, and be wide enough, if necessary, to carry a double line of railway. Not until 1861, however, had the necessary connections been laid in, with both the South Eastern and the Chatham lines, and with the consent of the Admiralty the first trains were running alongside the Channel steamers at Dover.

This introduces a fascinating piece of history. It was in 1855 that the East Kent Railway (four years later to become the London Chatham & Dover) obtained its powers to extend to Dover, and reached that town in 1861. Well before that date, and despite its shaky finances, the LCDR had been farseeing enough to institute enquiries as to the possible purchase of cross-Channel ships, and had even gone to the length of appointing a Naval

Architect! What the LCDR directors had in mind was to obtain the contract to carry the Anglo-French mail, which at that time was in the hands of a private firm. It was precisely at this time, in 1862, that the astute James Staats Forbes became General Manager of the Chatham Company.

Subsequent events played into his hands. In 1862 the Government decided to transfer the mail contract to rail transport, and offered it to the South Eastern Railway. This company, secure, as it thought, in the possession of its own prosperous Folkestone–Boulogne route, and foreseeing no profit worth mention in the mail contract, refused the offer. Forbes immediately stepped in, and obtained the contract for the Chatham line. What is more, in 1865 an agreement was reached between the two companies to pool the receipts from the Continental traffic, in the proportions of 63 per cent to the SER and 32 per cent to the LCDR at the start, but gradually dropping in the former case and rising in the latter until a 50: 50 basis was reached in 1872. How the South Eastern directors, with the receipts from their own port of Folkestone thrown into the pool, can have been so blind as to enter into such an agreement is a mystery indeed; they had plenty of cause to regret their decision before the fusion of the two companies in 1899.

▼ SS *Canterbury*, the only first class only ship ever built for the cross-Channel service, with the introduction of the "Golden Arrow" in 1929.   [British Railways

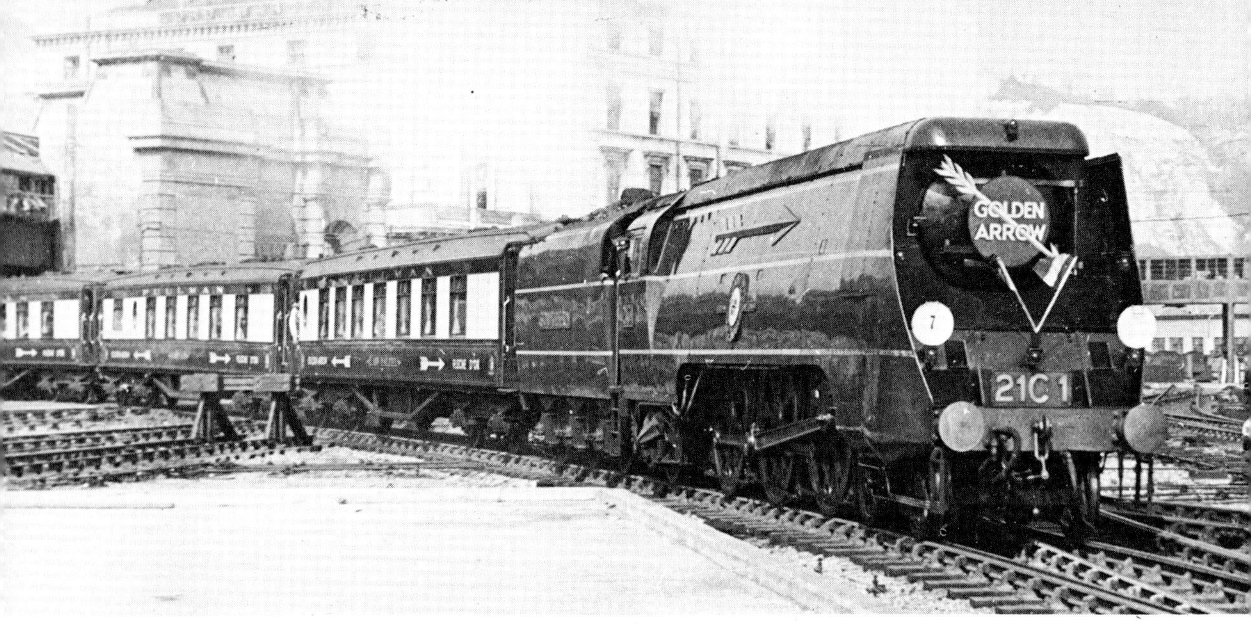

▲ The Pullman "Golden Arrow" drawing round the curve into Dover Marine, headed by Bulleid Pacific No. 21C1 *Channel Packet.*   [British Railways

▼ The capacious interior of Dover Marine station, with the "Golden Arrow" train at Platform 4.   [J. A. U. Woods

Not until 1864 did the two companies obtain powers to operate their own cross-Channel steamers. The Chatham bought up the steamers that were being operated by a firm named Churchward between Dover and Calais, and then began ordering new ships. Of these one of the most interesting was the *Calais-Douvres*, which entered service in 1878 with twin hulls 320ft long, and with twin paddle-wheels between them, the whole bridged by a main deck of considerable width, surmounted by four funnels. The twin hulls had a stabilising effect, which made the ship popular with travellers, but she was not easy to manoeuvre, and with her speed on 13 knots was heavy on coal. However, she operated successfully until 1878. In 1889 she was succeeded by a new *Calais-Douvres*, which once made the Dover–Calais crossing in 57min, at 22.6 knots. Fine ships were also being used by the South Eastern between Folkestone and Boulogne; and certain services were operated by the ships of the Northern Railway of France.

At the beginning of the present century turbine

▲ A down Continental express near Chelsfield, showing next the tender of No. 863 *Lord Rodney*, the luggage-boxes or containers which carried registered luggage throughout avoiding transhipment from train to ship and *vice versa*.   [F. R. Hebron

▼ An aerial view of the train-ferry dock at Dover.
[British Railways

propulsion was being introduced, and by 1907 five such ships—the *Queen, Onward, Invicta, Victoria* and *Empress*—had been added to the South Eastern & Chatham fleet. The 1914–1918 war took its toll of the SECR fleet, though to nothing like the same extent as the 1939–1945 war, and then, after the formation of the Southern Railway, there followed shipping developments of note. Two fine new ships, the *Isle of Thanet* and *Maid of Kent*, which entered service in 1925, were followed four years later by the *Canterbury*, of 2,910 gross tons, built to carry first class passengers only in connection with the new "Golden Arrow" service, connecting with all-Pullman trains on both sides of the water. But before many years had passed, air traffic was making such inroads on the cross-Channel railway receipts that an all-first-class service no longer could be justified, and in 1931 the "Golden Arrow" and the normal 11.00 service from Charing Cross were amalgamated and became available to both classes of passenger. Then came the interruption of the 1939–1945 war, which by sinkings cost the Southern Railway twelve ships in all; two of these were the *Maid of Kent* and the *Maid of Orleans*, that had been so familiar to cross-Channel passengers from Folkestone and Dover.

It was shortly before the 1914–1918 war that very important developments had been initiated at Dover Harbour. Changes had been planned considerably earlier, but had been held up in 1882 when the South Eastern & Channel Tunnel Company had been formed and had begun trial borings between Folkestone and Dover as a start to that great enterprise. As is common knowledge, owing to War Office opposition the plan failed to mature, but the borings had one unexpected result. They struck a seam of coal, and the result was the opening up of the Kent coalfield, with its pits at Betteshanger, Chilmanstone, Snowdown and Chislet, from which eventually good locomotive coal was supplied to the SECR and SR locomotive sheds at Dover and Ramsgate. Then in the late

1890s, when relations between Great Britain and both France and Germany were not of the best, the Government formed a plan for a strongly fortified harbour which would enclose the whole of Dover Bay and serve in future as a naval base of the greatest importance.

The South Eastern & Chatham Railway then changed its own Dover plans, which, in order to permit abandonment of the discomforts of the Admiralty Pier, were to construct a series of steamer berths spreading out from the shore in the form of an apron. Instead it was decided to build a new and commodious station, on reclaimed land, with ample quayage alongside, which would rival all other railway ports in the country in its facilities. So the work began in 1910 of building Dover Marine Station; it was badly held up by the 1914–1918 war, and though from 1915 onwards military use of the station became possible, it was not until 1919 that the travelling public was able to enjoy this vast improvement on the former discomforts of the Admiralty Pier.

Through all these years other services were being attracted to Dover as a port. In 1905 the first turbine steamer, the *Princesse Elizabeth*, was added to the Belgian Government's Ostend–Dover fleet, over a route which was rapidly becoming of considerable importance. Then in 1934 the Ostend fleet received another important addition, in the shape of the *Prince Baudouin*, the first cross-Channel ship to be driven by diesel engines, which gave her a speed of 25 knots.

In 1931 there entered service the Southern Railway SS *Autocarrier*, the first ship to be built expressly for the carriage of automobiles, of which 25 could be accommodated on board. Few could have anticipated the vast extent to which cross-Channel motor traffic would grow in later years, focussed mainly in the port of Dover.

As early as 1872 a Bill had been presented to Parliament for permission to ferry trains from Dover across the Channel, but had been rejected. The Channel Tunnel project then put this idea out of court for a good many years, and it was not until the 1914–1918 war that the first train-ferries began to operate, though not from Dover. They crossed from Richborough, a harbour just south of Ramsgate, to both Dunkerque and Calais, but exclusively for the carriage of war stores and munitions for the Forces. At last, however, a passenger train-ferry service became a reality in the year 1936. A new dock, 414ft long and 70ft wide, was built at Dover, and similar accommodation at Dunkerque, and three train-ferry ships, each capable of carrying 12 sleeping cars or similar length of wagons on three tracks, entered service; they were the *Hampton Ferry, Shepperton Ferry* and

▼ One of the earlier train-ferry ships operating between Dover and Calais, the SS *Shepperton Ferry.*
[British Railways

Twickenham Ferry. So, for the first time, the "Night Ferry" made it possible to travel without change in first class sleeping cars between Victoria and both Paris and Brussels.

Folkestone also in time acquired additional cross-Channel services. After the formation of the London Midland & Scottish Railway in 1923, the idea was conceived of using Tilbury as the port for a cross-Channel service to and from Dunkerque, using the French ship *Alsacien*, and this started in 1927. But little public interest was evinced, and owing largely to unpunctuality caused by fogs in the Thames estuary, in 1932 the ships were transferred to Folkestone which incidentally cut the sea crossing from $6\frac{1}{4}$ to $4\frac{1}{4}$hr. For a time three ships were employed, but the Dover–Dunkerque train-ferry brought this service to an end.

Another service which for a time used Folkestone as its port was that of the Zeeland Steamship Company of Holland. From 1876 this company worked a nightly service to and from Flushing, using a pier which the London Chatham & Dover Railway had built at Queenborough, in the Thames estuary at the mouth of the Medway, access to which was by a branch from Sittingbourne, on the Dover main line. This pier had a chequered history, as it was twice burned down, the second

▼ Through Paris sleeping cars being moved on to the *Shepperton Ferry* at Dover for their run across the Channel to Dunkerque. [British Railways

time in 1900, making necessary the temporary transfer of the Zeeland steamers to Port Victoria, on the opposite side of the Medway, reached by a direct branch from Gravesend.

Eventually, however, the Dutch line, hampered by the length of the crossing, the Thames fogs, and the poor pier facilities, decided to transfer from Queenborough to Folkestone, which it did in 1911. But the crossing was still too lengthy for effective competition with the Harwich–Hook of Holland route of the former Great Eastern Railway, and in 1927, by which time the GER had become absorbed in the London & North Eastern Railway, there was a second transfer, this time to Parkeston Quay. At first Flushing remained the Dutch port, but after the 1939–1945 war this was changed to the Hook of Holland, from which time the Zeeland ships provided the day service and the British ships the night service between Parkeston Quay and the Hook.

Reference is now needed to the marine activities of the London Brighton & South Coast Railway, which were on a smaller scale than those of the SECR but became in later years of no small importance. As far back as 1847, after having opened a branch from Lewes to Newhaven, the LBSCR obtained Parliamentary powers to own and operate steamships, though the first regular service between Newhaven and Dieppe was worked by a private firm called Maples & Morris, which

▲ Heaviest train on Southern metals—the "Night Ferry" from Dover to Victoria, headed by L1 class 4-4-0 No. 31753 and "Battle of Britain" Pacific No. 34066 *Spitfire*.

continued to function until 1867. In that year the LBSCR took over and also started a service of its own between Littlehampton and St. Malo, but it was the Newhaven–Dieppe service that was destined to become permanent. Powers were obtained in 1876 by the Brighton to acquire the property of the Newhaven Harbour Board, which, however, were not exercised, and it was the Newhaven Harbour Company that began in 1878 to transform the port, beginning with the construction of a new breakwater 2,800ft long, and a new east pier 1,500 ft long, which with many other improvements were completed in 1891. Not until 1926 did what by now had become the Southern Railway absorb the Newhaven Harbour Company, and initiate further improvements.

On the French side the Brighton's ally was the Western Railway of France, which ran a connecting service between Dieppe and Paris via Rouen, but owing to the much greater length of the Channel crossing—74 miles as compared with the 21 miles between Dover and Calais—the Newhaven–Dieppe route could never equal the SECR routes in the matter of time. Speed, however, was a distinguishing characteristic of the ships which plied from and to Newhaven. Some of these, it is interesting to note, were designed by William Stroudley, who combined with his *expertise* as the Brighton's Locomotive Superintendent a sound knowledge of naval architecture. Among his inventions were a very efficient type of feathering paddle-wheel, which added appreciably to the speed of the paddle-steamers.

The first turbine-driven ship on the service was the *Brighton*, which came into service in 1903 and had a maximum speed capacity of 21½ knots. Ten years later the new ship *Paris* raised the speed to 25 knots, and her arrival coincided with the opening, by the Western Railway of France, of a new direct route from Dieppe to Paris via Pontoise, avoiding Rouen, which by cutting 20 miles from the distance made possible a considerable acceleration of the service. There were few developments of note on the Newhaven–Dieppe route after the Southern Railway had taken over, and if its patronage by passengers to and from Paris has never been on a large scale, owing to the quicker journeys of its competitors, it has always been popular as a direct route to and from Normandy.

15 · *Southampton—Britain's Premier Port*

ONE OF THE greatest master-strokes in the entire history of the Southern Railway and its predecessors was the decision of the London & South Western Railway in 1892 to acquire the entire estate of the Southampton Dock Company. It was due to the enterprise of Charles Scotter, who in later years deservedly received a knighthood, and who after experience with the Manchester Sheffield & Lincolnshire Railway and particularly in the latter's marine activities at Hull and Grimsby had come to the LSWR in 1885 as General Manager. The Dock Company had strained its resources to the utmost in building the Empress Dock, which had been opened by Queen Victoria in 1890, and because it was unable to carry out further urgent work, particularly of dredging, the port had been falling into disrepute. One particularly bad blow had been in 1881, when the Peninsular & Oriental Company had abandoned Southampton in favour of the port of London. Little had been done by dredging to make Southampton accessible to the larger ships which were coming into service.

It was in these circumstances that the London & South Western Railway, which was one of the Dock Company's biggest creditors, stepped in and negotiated a purchase that the railway was never likely to regret. No time was lost in transforming the port. Dredging began at once, and within a year the Inman Line had transferred its Transatlantic steamers from Liverpool to Southampton, at the same time changing its name to the America Line. This was the first of a series of triumphs that Southampton was to achieve at the expense of Merseyside. By 1897 the Royal Mail, Union and Castle Lines were all operating to and from Southampton, together with the German Hamburg-America and North German Lloyd Lines, the Dutch Nederland and Rotterdam-Lloyd Lines, the General Steam Navigation and various minor companies. Such were the immediate effects of the change in ownership of Southampton Docks that in no more than six months of Scotter's energetic management passenger receipts had increased by 25 per cent, those from imports by 32 per cent, and those from exports by no less than 36 per cent.

The dredging, of course, was only the beginning of changes that were to be revolutionary indeed. An extensive area known locally as the "Mudlands", at the mouth of the Test, was reclaimed; and new quays were provided, as well as an Ocean Dock, with depths of water from 28ft to 32ft. It may be noted that the head of Southampton Water has always had the benefit of double tides, and this has limited the amount of dredging needed to accommodate the largest vessels. By 1895 the Prince of Wales Dry Dock was opened, 750ft long, 87ft wide at the entrance and 112ft wide at the coping; but this was eclipsed ten years later by the crowning achievement of Scotter's reign, which was the bringing into service of the largest graving dock in the world, 875ft long, 90ft wide at the entrance and 125ft at the coping. This Trafalgar Dry Dock had a capacity well in advance of any ships then afloat. As these port facilities improved, so did the attraction of Southampton; gradually the Cunard and White Star liners were attracted

▼ Southampton's Ocean Dock, from the air. The ships seen are the SS *Empress of Britain*, left; the SS *Olympic* in the Ocean Dock, centre; and the SS *Mauretania* in the floating dock, extreme right.

[British Railways

▲ The Ocean Quay at Southampton; the SS *Queen
Mary* is seen in the King George V graving dock
(lower right).   [British Railways

away from Liverpool, as Southampton had the
additional advantage that ships based there could
tap the European traffic directly by crossing the
Channel to make calls at Cherbourg. Equally the
ships of the French Line were soon making calls at
Southampton on their way from Cherbourg to the
United States.

Looking on into the future, the Southern
Railway soon after its formation began to plan
further developments of the port which would
involve expenditure on such a scale that the SR
Board and Sir Herbert Walker, who now occupied
the managerial chair, needed considerable courage
in authorising the scheme. First there arrived in
1924 by water the world's largest floating dock,
960ft long and 130ft wide, which had been ordered
by the London & South Western Railway and
towed from the Tyne, where it was built. Next
came the most ambitious plan of all. It was to
reclaim a further 400 acres of the "Mudlands" in

order to provide a new Ocean Quay $1\frac{1}{2}$ miles long,
capable of accommodating simultaneously six of
the world's biggest liners. At the inner end of this
was to be a new graving dock which again would
claim a world record.

In 1927 the work began of dredging the muddy
flats and depositing the excavated material in a kind
of dam across the mouth of the bay; when
20,000,000 tons had thus been tipped and
strengthened with concrete, the water behind the
dam was pumped out until the area was dry, and
some 2,000,000 tons of concrete were then used in
the building of the new quay and the new graving
dock, the latter 1,200ft long and 135ft across.
Alongside the quay, which had a depth of water of
35ft, a fine range of station buildings was erected,
with every possible facility for handling passengers
and freight and direct railway access. It was a
great day in Southern Railway history when in
1933 the Royal yacht entered the new King George
V Dry Dock and it was declared open by King
George V in person.

All the world's largest and fastest liners were
now being seen regularly at Southampton, and their
names conjure up a host of memories—the
Lusitania, Mauretania, Aquitania, Majestic, Titanic,
to name but a few—and finally the record-breaking
Queen Mary and *Queen Elizabeth,* the two last-
mentioned each requiring three boat trains to carry
their passengers and luggage from and to Waterloo.
At the maximum, the ships of some thirty companies were using Southampton regularly. Then
came the interruption of the 1939–1945 war, when
Southampton was under severe enemy attack by
bombing, and for the time being the ocean traffic
was virtually suspended. In view of the damage
sustained by the port, recovery took time; since
then the most notable development, helped by the
fact that certain buildings bordering the Ocean
Dock had been destroyed, has been their replacement by the magnificent Ocean Terminal building,
under the auspices of British Rail.

Throughout the period that has been described
there were steamer services of the London & South
Western and Southern Railways that themselves
were based on Southampton. As far back as 1848
the LSWR obtained Parliamentary powers to own
and operate steamships, and in that year the railway
took over from the South Western Steam Navigation Company the mail services from Southampton
to the Channel Islands, and also to Havre and St.
Malo in France. These were being operated on
certain days of the week only, but gradually were
expanded; in 1864 passengers for the first time

were able to embark at the Docks rather than in unsheltered conditions on the Royal Pier, but it was not until 1890 that the first twin-screw ships, capable of 19½ knots, entered service, to and from the Channel Islands, and immediately proved popular. It may be added that the LSWR was sharing with the Great Western Railway in the service to and from the Channel Islands, in the latter case from and to Weymouth; the ships sailed three times weekly on alternate nights during the winter, but daily by each route in the summer season. By 1911 thirteen LSWR ships were engaged on the Channel crossings. From 1894

there was a considerable improvement also in the service between Southampton and Havre. The dangerous reefs which guard the islands took their toll, especially in foggy weather, and two ships were lost in this way, while four more were sunk in the 1914–1918 war by enemy action.

After the Southern Railway had taken over, a number of new and bigger ships were introduced, two 325ft in length for the Southampton–St. Malo service in 1924. For some years this service continued to run at times which varied with the tides, but the completion of a new harbour at St. Malo in 1931 made it possible from then on to

▲ The modern Ocean Terminal, Southampton, with the SS *Queen Elizabeth*.   [British Railways

▼ A boat train with passengers off the SS *Queen Mary* leaving Southampton Ocean Terminal for Waterloo, behind 4-6-0 No. 30853 *Sir Richard Grenville*.

[B. A. Butt

▲ Some of the American-built 0-6-0 shunters, bought by the SR in 1946 for Southampton Docks shunting work. [R. Sherlock

▲ A Channel Islands boat train making its way through Weymouth streets with diesel haulage to the ship. [J. Scrace

operate at regular sailing times. The years 1928 and 1931 saw three fine new ships, each 306ft long, introduced to the Channel Islands service. At various other periods the Southern operated both passenger and freight steamers between South-ampton and the French ports of Cherbourg and Caen.

Brief reference is now needed to the minor maritime activities of the Southern Railway and the former London & South Western Railway. The principal communication to and from the Isle of Wight has always been the shuttle steamer service between Portsmouth Harbour and Ryde, operated jointly by the LSWR and the London Brighton & South Coast Railway. At the grouping the SR took over five paddle steamers, ranging in age from 12 to 34 years; another joined them in 1924, two more in 1930 and a fourth in 1937. A new departure in 1927 was the inauguration of a service for motorcars between Portsmouth and a new slipway at Fishbourne, just west of Ryde, which by 1930 was using three diesel-driven ferries. Then the west end of the island was served by another ferry, which plied across the Solent between Lymington Pier and Yarmouth. The long narrow estuary of the River Lymington, used by these ships, needs careful navigation, and the diesel-driven *Lymington*, which entered service in 1938, had no rudders but propellers of which the pitch was controllable from the bridge, so enabling her to be moved sideways from the narrow berth at Lymington.

It may be added that there was at one time yet another crossing from the mainland to the Isle of Wight. In 1863 a branch line was opened from Gosport, on the then Fareham & Gosport line, to a new pier at Stokes Bay on the Spithead, im-mediately opposite Ryde. At first an independent company provided the ships, but in 1875 the LSWR took over. Although this was the shortest crossing, the service could never compete effectively with that to and from Portsmouth Harbour, because of the latter's much superior railway connections. At the beginning of the 1914–1918 war the Stokes Bay service was suspended, and the taking over by the Admiralty in 1922 of the branch and pier brought it to an end. Another route was that always taken by Queen Victoria on her journeys to and from Osborne House; she used to embark at Gosport for Cowes, but this never became a public service.

In conclusion, it is worth while to review the immense size to which the Southern Railway fleet had grown in the middle 1930s, which may be regarded as its heyday, before air competition had begun seriously to affect its patronage. Between Dover, Folkestone, Calais and Boulogne there were seven passenger ships, one Autocarrier, and seven cargo ships. Between Newhaven and Dieppe, owned jointly by the SR and the French State Railway (successor to the Western), seven passenger and four cargo ships were in service. Trading between Southampton and the Channel Islands, Havre, Cherbourg and St. Malo required eleven passenger and six cargo vessels. Between Portsmouth and the Isle of Wight could be found seven passenger ships and three motor ferries, supplemented by two passenger ships and four tugs between Lymington and Yarmouth. Various smaller vessels completed this imposing fleet. But Southampton was always by far the most valuable of the maritime possessions of the Southern Railway.